PERSPECTIVES ON
ENGINEERING

By Richard H. Spencer and Raymond E. Floyd

authorHOUSE®

AuthorHouse™
1663 Liberty Drive
Bloomington, IN 47403
www.authorhouse.com
Phone: 1-800-839-8640

First published by AuthorHouse 6/17/2011

ISBN: 978-1-4634-1091-9 (e)
ISBN: 978-1-4634-1092-6 (dj)
ISBN: 978-1-4634-1093-3 (sc)

Library of Congress Control Number: 2011910549

Printed in the United States of America

Table of Contents

Preface

The reader of this book will find no equations, algorithms, data tables or graphs, that can be found in most Engineering texts. Rather than such material, the reader will find aspects of Engineering that are not taught as a part of theory courses or in the Engineering course curriculum. The authors write from personal experience as engineers in a laboratory environment and progressing through an extensive sequence of positions, i.e. Lab engineers, first, second, and third level managers. We were also sent to other locations, including European lab's as experts in specialized technical areas. This book is based on those personal qualifications, and not on any references to other's work although there are some suggested other readings that may expand on a particular topic. The information presented in the following pages is that learned in over 100 years of combined experience of the authors, things the authors learned, practiced as engineers, and managers of engineers, programmers, and technicians. Experience gained in conveying information to higher management, in good times and bad.

The idea for the book grew out of a number of conference papers, industrial publication articles, and several articles published or in review by the IEEE in their *Potentials* magazine. In each of the articles and papers, we attempted to convey some of our experiences to help young engineers understand the requirements that would be placed on them to perform in industry once they left the structured environment of academia. To that end, we believe we have provided that insight, and hope other aspiring engineers can benefit from our perspectives.

Chapter 1 - Engineering 101

Over the years of our careers, we have been asked many times by students, employees, and peers at management meetings, what approaches to our assignments as engineers or as managers served us best. While there was always a short time to think about the question, the answer was almost always the same, whether one follows a technical career, a career in management, or a mix of both. The secret is to keep things simple (more about that later):

- be considerate of others feelings and abilities,
- be consistent when dealing with people not favoring one over another,
- maintain sensitivity to others as there may be pressures they are under that you are not aware of, and
- do the very best job you can, always striving to be as competent as you can within your abilities.

The impact of each part of this answer is important to understand, as both the positive and negative aspects can affect not only your career, but the career of others.

Basics

In moving from the world of academia into the world of industry, there are many adaptations that will have to be made. In school a failure on a test can be a transient action, perhaps lowering a grade point average, possibly requiring a course to be repeated, or simply an action lost in the semester's average and of little consequence. In industry, failure on a test can be a very large loss of time and equipment – all of which is quickly equated to the bottom line as a loss in revenue or to the annual budget. In most instances, the young engineer will be provided some level of guidance – protection against the possibility of catastrophic failure early in the engineer's career. Academia provides the fundamentals and introductory tools for the engineer, but it is the application of that knowledge and those tools within the industrial environment that will define the success or failure of an engineering career.

By some interpretations, these approaches are simply the old fashion common rules of courtesy or manners. Before too strong of an exception is taken to the comment of "old fashion", look around and see how many examples of poor manners, or lack of courtesy, can be observed in a day. The list, unfortunately, is very long. Consider people failing to hold doors for others, even for their own family members, cutting into lines, yelling at clerks in a store, yelling or gesturing at other drivers, or simple acts of rudeness, and the list goes on. When looking at applications within the work environment, how many times do you hear "Thank you" when you hand in a report you were asked to complete, or you say to someone who gives you your tickets for a trip? Even considering that the work may be within the expected assignment, what is the impact of such simple words? In those two words, you are demonstrating consideration for the other person's time on your behalf. On the other side, how about the remark, "That's the dumbest idea I have ever heard", given by a peer or even a manager in a discussion. It may be the dumbest idea ever, but the remark itself is probably right next to the dumb idea as being out of line. Being embarrassed in front of one's peers by a peer or manager is among the worst things that can happen to an individual.

Sensitivity training is one of the more important sessions covered in modern manager training classes. It is seldom discussed during academic courses, unless there is a team effort involved. Even then, since most such team efforts are short term, the expedient solution to a problem may be to simply reassign the offending team member to a new team to resolve the problem. Little discussion is entered into about the role of being sensitive to the needs of others. In particular are the current topical lessons covering sexual harassment, where ignoring such rules can result in a career ending termination. The need for sensitivity goes far beyond just sexual harassment. It applies to anyone's feelings, beliefs, or personal traits that could cause anguish, pain, or embarrassment for that person if discussed in public. Understanding events, pressures, and other circumstances involving co-workers or others with whom you have to interface expose you to areas where you must be fine tuned to other people's feelings, and that may be uncomfortable to you. It may not always be comfortable, but the more sensitive you are in dealing with other people's needs, the more successful you will be in your own career. The use of sarcasm offers one of the greatest opportunities for exposure to insensitivity. Quick, cutting remarks may seem funny at the time, but in retrospect may cross the line, causing peer to peer working relationship problems. The use of sarcasm by a manager to peer could even be worse. A few sarcastic remarks flung in your direction makes you feel diminished and less willing to work with, or for, the individual attacking you (verbally of course).

Being consistent in how you approach work, deal with people, handle various situations, and even how you handle your boss can go a long way to ensure a successful career. Being consistent says that assignments are completed on time and satisfactorily, providing indications that you can be depended on. While this trait is important to the average engineer, it is critical as a manager. For example, if a manager is inconsistent in handling job evaluations the word will get around that, "The boss sure takes care of his, or her, favorites." Just the hint of being inconsistent can destroy the credibility of the manager in the eyes of his, or her, staff. This does not mean that the expectations of a group of personnel are all the same. There are different skill sets, levels of experience, and a number of other items that may change the level of *expectation* between individuals. Such expectations, based on the skills of the individual, applied consistently across the staff will be recognized and appreciated by those being directed by the manager. This can become even more critical when peers, having worked together for a number of years, suddenly experience that great schism – one of them is promoted to the position of manager of the group and is now the boss. Now the new manager must address personnel issues, performance problems, salary adjustments, and a host of other items that prior to the move into management weren't of concern.

In addressing competence, one would hope that you may rise within an organization based on your demonstrated ability. However, having said that, perhaps best known commentary is from Dr. L. J. Peter's statement in his 1968 book, *The Peter Principle*, concerning a person's ability to rise within the business world; "In a hierarchy every employee tends to rise to his or her level of incompetence." If you are comfortable in rising to your level of incompetence, so be it. Having said that, be sure to get out of the way. There are others who will have no more competence than you do, however, they are willing to research, learn, and adapt their knowledge to new situations and opportunities. They may not be the greatest researcher, board designer, chip designer, and so forth, but they can gain sufficient knowledge to understand the concepts being employed. Their *adaptation* is the very strength that will allow them to continue to rise within the hierarchy – in spite of their perceived level of incompetence. They follow another old saying in the business world, "Lead, follow, or get out of the way!"

Accept No Limits

Another area to remain aware of in industry is to remain cognizant of events around you and the effect those events will have. Don't become a creature of habit, break out of that day-to-day paradigm and do something to benefit man-kind! Consider that whimsical character of imagination Don Quixote de la Mancha, the lead in the stage play Man of La Mancha, as he sings the familiar words:

To dream the impossible dream
To fight the unbeatable foe
To bear with unbearable sorrow
To run where the brave dare not go.

We are not suggesting the young engineer joust with windmills, or attempt to right all the wrongs in our world. Each of us has the ability to examine what is going on around us, and through a personal paradigm shift, work toward a better tomorrow. A few brief examples will help identify such dreamers and their impact on history.

Around 1490, an Italian sailor was laughed at, and some even called him mad. His vision was to sail westward from the European continent, westward until he could circumnavigate his way to India and the rich spice trade. He believed the earth was round, against the popular belief of the majority of people, and that he should be able to make such a journey. The rest is history, as children recite each year, "In 1492 Columbus sailed the ocean blue", and the exploits of Christopher Columbus and his three ships are remembered. His journey took more than 60 days, certainly causing concern among his crewman and shipmates, but he believed and achieved his dream with the discovery of the New World. While it was not quite the discovery of a new route to India he had envisioned, the impact to the world has certainly been noted.

Moving forward in time, the year is 1903. The day is blustery, overcast, with a stiff breeze coming in from the Atlantic Ocean. That day saw the culmination of the work and dreams of Orville and Wilbur Wright, credited with the first heavier-than-air human flight on December 17, 1903. While most people are aware of their accomplishment, few understand the real accomplishment the Wright brothers had achieved. Many inventors had attempted powered flying before the Wright brothers, all had failed. Why? The concepts involved with wing design were well understood, and what appeared as the major problem was the motor power being applied to make each design lift itself from the earth and soar into the sky – each attempt ending in failure and, sometimes, death for the inventor. The Wright brothers were owners of a very successful bicycle shop, repairing and selling bicycles. They had an avid interest in manned flight, but it was far removed from their daily activities involved with bicycles. In their time, they examined the aircraft wing design and decided that there were sufficient designs in existence to support heavier-than-air flight, whether trying to mimic the wing of a bird, or simply designed to provide lift across its upper surface. They also determined that more power was not the answer to the problem of manned flight, the amount of power to pull or push the airplane sufficiently fast to generate the lift was quiet small. From their perspective, they needed a paradigm shift to investigate what they envisioned as the principle problem for successful manned flight – control. Orville and Wilbur took some of their bicycle experience and applied it to the control problem. From their experience, you did not simply turn the front wheel to the left to turn left, but included moving your body to the right at the same time to counter the forces trying to spill you onto the ground. They extended those simple concepts into a three dimensional solution of control for roll, pitch, and yaw for the aircraft. The Wright brothers were granted patent #821,393 in 1906 for their "Flying Machine", just the beginning of the wonders of flight and another impossible dream come to past.

Moving the calendar forward to the mid-1950's and we find the United States bitterly divided in terms of equal rights and segregation. Through a number of decisions by the Supreme Court concerning education, voting rights, and other issues, a movement began to help break the barriers of race, and build toward a better day. One citizen believing strongly in the need for equal rights for all citizens was Dr. Martin Luther King. He was an activist, participating in marches, demonstrations, and civil disobedience. Of the many speeches Dr. King delivered, it is the one he gave in 1963 on the steps of the Lincoln Memorial in Washington, D.C. that is best remembered, his dream of what could be, as noted in the following excerpt:

> I have a dream that one day this nation will rise up and live out the true meaning of its creed, "We hold these truths to be self-evident, that all men are created equal. I have a dream that one day on the red hills of Georgia, the sons of former slaves and the sons of former slave owners will be able to sit down together at the table of brotherhood.
>
> ...
>
> I have a dream today.

His dream may not be totally realized yet, but without his vision and dream, nothing would have been done.

A few years later, a young, new president told the nation, "I believe this nation should commit itself to achieving the goal, before the decade is out, of landing a man on the moon and returning him safely to earth." With those words, President John F. Kennedy set in motion a vast network of engineers, machinists, scientists, literally tens of thousands of workers with a single goal – to send astronauts to the moon and safely return them. As young men, we watched the Freedom Seven Mercury astronauts make the first steps in the United States space program with their sub-orbital and short term orbital flights. The Mercury flights were followed by the Gemini series with its twelve flights, each moving the program closer to the ultimate goal – APOLLO. By the time APOLLO arrived, author Floyd was fortunate to be a member of the launch team, supporting test and launch activities at the Kennedy Space Center in Florida. The synergy of the people and companies involved was magnificent. Company A didn't have a problem during the launch countdown, the launch support team had a problem, one which everyone stood ready to help solve. When the APOLLO 1 crew of Grissom, Chaffee, and White were lost, the entire team suffered as if it had lost a member of the family. It went beyond a job, beyond being a member of a team, it truly seemed more like a family, all with a common goal. And when APOLLO 13 uttered those famous words, "Houston, we have a problem.", the intensity of the workers in searching for solutions for the safe return of the spacecraft crew is truly hard to imagine. When Neil Armstrong said, "One small step for man, one giant leap for mankind.", he spoke for all of us who had been part of the dream set in place some eight years before.

Explorer, inventor, political activist, President, and astronauts – all unique and different, yet an underlying commonality of looking at things as they were and wanting something better, each having their own impossible dream. They were able to make the paradigm shift needed to achieve their dream. Having the dream in itself is not enough. As Lao Tzu once said, "A journey of a thousand miles begins with a single step", the challenge is moving from the dream to reality.

And the world will be better for this
That one man, scorned and covered with scars
Still strove with his last ounce of courage
To reach the unreachable star.

Changing Paths

Spencer, who has an electrical engineering degree, had been promoted once, and was the lead test engineer on an essentially mechanical printer that had several human interaction interfaces. Having seen some of the laboratory's test operators having problems dealing with these, he had concern about customer machine operator's ability to deal with those with reasonable ease and accuracy. (Spencer had a pre-test lab background in the field, servicing company machines in the customer offices.)

The company had just hired a PhD specialist in Human Factors Engineering. Spencer called on him to observe the printer, and discuss his concerns. The upshot, as to the printer, was that Spencer's concerns were validated by the Human Factors expert. Shortly thereafter Spencer was requested to transfer to the company's Development Laboratory, at that site, to work with the PhD in establishing a Human Factors Engineering Laboratory. Other PhDs were brought in, and some engineers from the development departments. After about three years the new human factors engineering team was working smoothly. Spencer requested transfer back to the Testing Laboratory where he could apply much of what he had learned to the testing of machines and systems.

There, Spencer was promoted into his first department management position. A couple of years later he was requested to act as the team leader in assessing usability of a system being developed across laboratories in several different company locations. Later, he transferred to another state as part of a laboratory startup team for a new company site where a new plant was being built. This entailed going to the architect's offices and illustrating changes he identified as being required to provide a satisfactory testing laboratory, many of which had nothing directly to do with having a degree in electrical engineering. What did apply, was the way of thinking, and looking at things through the eyes of an engineer.

Other Readings

"Christopher Columbus: Explorer", http://www.enchantedlearning.com

"John F. Kennedy and the Space Program", http://www.uah.edu

King, Rev. Martin Luther. (1963). *"I Have A Dream"*, http://www. usconstitution.net

"The Impossible Dream". From Man of La Mancha, music by Mitch Leigh and lyrics by Joe Dorian. http://www.reelclassics.com

"The Wright Brothers & The Invention of the Aviation Age", http://www. nasm.st.edu

Floyd, R. (1993). *"The Four "Ins" of Management – Avoid Them!"*, Industrial Management, May/June 1993.

Floyd, R. (2008). *"Rules of Thumb"*, IEEE Potentials, November/ December 2008.

Floyd, R. (2011). *"On Planning Your Career"*, IEEE Potentials, May/ June 2011.

Floyd, R. (2011), *"Chef, Cook, or Bottle Washer?"*, IEEE Potentials, May/ June 2011.

Spencer, R. (1983). *"Planning, Implementing, and Control in Product Test and Assurance"*, Prentice-Hall, Inc. Upper Saddle River, NJ.

Chapter 2 – Engineering Specialties

Over many years the authors have known people who had enrolled in an engineering curriculum, then decided that was not what they really wanted to do. Also there were those who switched their engineering major when they decided there were conditions they preferred to work with that may not be available in their planned field. For instance, one decided he would prefer to work outside, not in a laboratory or office, so switched from chemical to petroleum engineering curriculum, with the expectation that the new choice would have greater opportunity for outside work. Such changes are not uncommon, but the student must realize that the change may be costly, both in time and money. Depending on when the change is made, the degree completion may be pushed beyond the expected four years by two or more years – and suffer considerable additional costs.

It is interesting to talk to young people, high school seniors and college freshmen, and discuss with them the course of study they plan to follow in college and for their career. Frequently, an individual will simply say, "I'm going into Engineering." That is somewhat akin to saying trees are green – there is such a variation in what an engineer is, what courses need to be studied, what the interests of the student are, what jobs are available to the graduate, and the list goes on and on. If the individual can narrow the choice, even slightly, to say, "I'm going to be an electrical engineer." there remains a large number of choices to be made as one embarks on the studies needed for the new career.

Over the years of work as engineers we have seen many engineering graduates who have specialized so severely that they proved to be unable to adapt for success in some very challenging opportunities. One case in point was a young engineer trained in electronics, but unable to handle testing of printers. Why? The testing involved primarily mechanical components, although much of the printer itself contained electronics for paper advance, hammer firing, data transfer, and so forth, but he couldn't adapt to the *system* aspects of the job. After a time he left and found a new position in aircraft cockpit simulators, although we suspect he didn't last there either, as there are many, if not more, mechanical aspects he would have to learn. A second case was a bright young engineer carrying a 4.0 GPA, and appeared to have a brilliant future as a design engineer – until he was asked to perform a simple modification of a printed circuit card. In all of his training, he had never soldered on a circuit board – *and had no interest in learning.* He moved on, looking for opportunities in research and development where he hoped to apply the theory he had learned. In his case, we wished him luck, but doubted his future success simply because of his attitude toward the mundane aspects of the work – he hadn't come to the realization that every project is not going to be involved in startling new discoveries, there will be those times when the work is very plain. Other young engineers who had adequate electrical, electronics, and mechanical training were most often very successful in design, and/or test of a wide variety of business machines and systems. Some expanded their career opportunities by also becoming adept at programming for testing and manufacturing process control.

On the other hand, there are those who want to do research in highly specialized or specific areas. In that case specialization may be appropriate, as long as the individual recognizes the possible limitations being placed on their career path through such narrow focus. The authors, however, write from years of experience in the testing of a wide variety of business machines, robots, automated manufacturing systems, human factors assessments, and various systems, ranging from office systems to others for airports, parking lots, trucking centers, and highway applications. In such cases, the engineer must be able to understand the *system* aspects of the application, installation, and, if required, provide operating instructions that the non-technical operator can understand and follow quickly and correctly. Yes, the engineer must also develop good communication and writing skills along the way, and certainly the ability to work with others in a cooperative and courteous manner.

One author, Spencer, who had several years experience as a combat cameraman and experience in a hand-cast aluminum cooking ware factory, decided to acquire an Electrical Engineering degree. He was offered positions at a television company, the U.S. Geodetic Survey Service, missile research, and IBM. He settled on IBM and had a very satisfying 38 year career there, spending the major part of that time within the Product Test function. In that role, he was charged with the testing of new products prior to public announcement or shipment, and tested everything from input/output equipment to mainframes – mechanical and electrical. While in the university he gave special attention to mechanical areas of study and to technical writing; aiming for understandability by non-engineers. Later at IBM, he had many technical reports to write, coached other engineers and programmers in writing for understandability by non-engineer product users, had two books on product testing published, and was assigned to rewrite a management manual.

The other author, also with an Electrical Engineering degree, gained experience in radar, field engineering, and programming prior to starting his career at IBM. Based on his broad based experience, he was tasked with designing, proposing to NASA management for funding and approval, and finally writing, integrating, and testing procedures for diagnostic programs for support computers at the Kennedy Space Center in Florida. During his IBM career, he worked in missile support, Product Test, and automated manufacturing systems design. During a 26 year period with IBM, the authors spent many years working together, often on the same projects involving work not only in the laboratory, but also in the field, in the USA and abroad; even involved with the testing of an anti-collision system aboard ships for the shipping industry.

In other words, it is well for many young engineers to approach their training with an open mind about what they will learn and decide if specialization is meant for them. If not, they need to be able to adapt to a wide variety of opportunities over a range of engineering capabilities. By such an approach they may find there are many more opportunities to take advantage of as they progress in their careers. In addition, with a broad outlook, the young engineers may find more opportunities to move into and become successful managing a broad range of engineering projects and engineering personnel. Engineering over specialization can restrict the young engineer's opportunities – perhaps they should try for a little broader approach to provide the greatest opportunity.

While it would take a fairly large book to discuss all of the variations of engineering studies, within this text some insight will be provided into the types of studies required for general engineering, and some specifics for a few more clearly defined engineering occupations (and even those few may have enough variation to cause confusion.) It is also important to note that engineering studied in the United States may be significantly different when considering other nations and the curriculum implemented within their schools.

Basic Engineering Skill Needs

To begin, the student should have a high interest in science and mathematics. High school courses should have included basic math, algebra, trigonometry, and geometry. In addition, one or two classes in chemistry and physics are essential. In general, a college curriculum in the engineering path will require the student to include such courses as college algebra, trigonometry, calculus (integral and differential), physics, and strength of materials, with most of these classes coming during the first two years. More specific specialization will more often come in the final two years of study. Added to these are other science, humanities, and communication courses required for accreditation, and the list of required courses is quite extensive. The Technology Accreditation Commission (TAC) and the Accreditation Board for Engineering and Technology (ABET), also referred to TAC/ABET, has very specific requirements for accreditation of school programs, both in technical content and humanities content. In general, 1/3 of the total required hours must be in the technical specialization, but no more than 2/3, with the remaining hours reserved for the science, humanities, and communication course requirements. For those readers who may not be aware of the TAC/ABET role in education, they provide ac-creditation reviews for school programs in engineering and engineering technology, both in the United States and other countries. It should be noted, that TAC/ABET are not the only accreditation bodies, but the most prominent in the United States for engineering and engineering technology.

The student may also be able to exercise an option to take either an engineering degree program, or an engineering technology degree pro-gram. In most cases, the engineering degree will have greater emphasis on mathematics and design courses, while the engineering technology will have greater emphasis on labs and general technical studies. While both degrees are in engineering, the first would be more inclined to work in design or research, while the latter would more often be found in field support, manufacturing, and product test. As noted earlier, the list of "engineering degrees" is quite large, ranging from microbiology, to computers, to mechanical, civil, electrical, aeronautical,..., and the list goes on. In the following pages, some of the more typical engineering career fields will be examined, and some of the choices offered will be discussed. <u>Regardless of the technical path, the ability to write and speak clearly and understandably by various levels of others is essential.</u>

Electrical Engineering

When one hears that someone is an electrical engineer, the first thought may be that the person is involved in computer design, i.e. a digital design engineer. Just as easily, the thought may encompass the work of a power engineer, or radio frequency engineer, and the list goes on across many different fields – all associated with electrical engineering. These thoughts just scratch the surface of what an electrical engineer may be trained to do. While the computer industry does use a large number of electrical engineers, not all are involved in digital design. Many will be involved in power supply design, analog equipment design, and peripheral equipment design (such as disks, memories, tape units, and printers). Some may also be found in the design of wide area network equipment, converters, modems, and other associated equipment.

Beyond the computer industry, electrical engineers may be found in the communications industry, designing and testing line amplifiers, transmitters, receivers, modems, and wide area network components (note the crossover in engineering applications from the computer industry into communications.) In addition, communication industry electrical engineers may specialize in radio frequency technology, thus being employed in radio and radar applications, or even satellite communications.

Another area that employs many electrical engineers is the power industry. Here, the emphasis is on the generation and distribution of electrical power – power used by industry and the private sectors. The engineers in this case are trained in AC power generation and distribution, and, frequently, have more training in the design and use of electric motors and generators. One industry that uses motor designers is the petroleum industry, where motors are designed as submersible units to provide the power needed to lift the crude oil from the well to the surface. Of course, submersible motors are not the only motors used in the petroleum industry, nor are they the only application found in motors across many industries. As part of the power industry sector, the engineer may also have additional training in the development of solar cell technology and wind turbines.

The electrical engineer may also pick up programming experience along the way, experience used to support the mechanical engineer in the design of automated manufacturing tools. The programming may be on devices used to control machine automation, like a programmable logic controller (PLC), where the programming language may be a special application language like LabView* for control of the device, or it may be assembler, BASIC, or C++ in the event a PC is used as the controlling device.

Mechanical Engineering

Mechanical engineering is as diverse as electrical engineering. In this case, the mechanical engineer may be concerned with structural engineering, i.e. buildings, bridges, roads, where the concern is in loading and structural integrity. The courses of interest will be strength of materials and physics of forces acting on structures.

As noted in the electrical engineering section, mechanical engineers are also heavily involved in the petroleum industry, designing the pumps that provide the lift needed to bring the crude oil from the well to the surface (powered by the electric motors mentioned previously). Not only do the pumps have to provide lift, the materials and surface treatments must be selected by the engineer to survive in a very hostile environment – heat, pressure, and corrosive liquids. From that, the mechanical engineer must be trained in the reaction of metals to corrosive liquids, a crossover into the chemical industry.

Factory automation depends heavily on the mechanical engineer, where the machines to build components, sub-assemblies, and final assembly are typically designed by the mechanical engineer (with help from the electrical engineer and programmer). One class, or classes, most typically found in the mechanical engineering curriculum will be computer aided drawing, or CAD, offered in either two dimensional programs or the newer three dimensional modeling techniques such as SolidWorks.

The power industry also calls heavily on the mechanical engineer, where the towers for transmission lines must be designed to support the power lines, supporting in all types of weather and other adverse conditions such as icing, high winds, and large temperature ranges. In addition, the physical structures such as dams, spillways, generator housings, etc. are all within the purview of the mechanical and civil engineer.

Chemical Engineering

Besides the mathematics and physics, chemical engineers should also enjoy both organic and inorganic chemistry studies. If they enjoy organic chemistry the most, typical jobs will be found in the oil industry as a petroleum engineer, applications engineer, corrosive engineer, and similar job titles. They may also find themselves employed within the chemical industry, involved in the development and manufacture of such products as rubber, tires, carbon black, and fuel oils and gases.

If the student's interests and studies lean more to the inorganic side, the job opportunities can overlap the organic side, with employment in the chemical industry involved in the development of new materials, additives, exotic chemical mixtures, and so forth, i.e. soaps, cleaning materials and other similar products. The inorganic chemical engineer may also find interesting work in the development of new metal mixtures, where the new mix may provide better life in corrosive environments, have higher temperature characteristics, or more malleable under certain stress conditions. Many new materials found in use in the various space programs are the result of chemical engineering discoveries.

Manufacturing Engineering

The manufacturing engineer, sometimes called an industrial engineer, is primarily concerned with the movement of products through the manufacturing floor from raw parts to finished product. The concerns cover the movement of parts from inventory to the proper point on the manufacturing floor, to the generation of operator assembly procedures, to the proper functioning of manufacturing tools, and to the routing of the product as it progresses through the entire manufacturing process (product routing). Specific tools needed by the operator will also be identified and/or designed by the manufacturing engineer. Assembly procedures will be studied and time-in-motion studies carried out to ensure the procedures embody the most efficient manner of assembly possible – to quote the old adage, "Time is money".

Computer Engineering

The field of computer engineering is another one of those careers that may take one of two very divergent paths. The first path is into the design of new computer systems, where the design is more involved with new application specific integrated circuits (ASIC), new methods of using multiple processors for increased throughput, ever decreasing circuit spacing within the chip designs, and similar activities aimed at new computer designs. The second path is more along the lines of designing new operating systems that provide real-time process support, multi-processor support, and new applications for the average user. In the first path, the program will more than likely be referred to as computer engineering, while the second path may be called computer science. The first path will be more oriented to digital and analog circuit design with courses and labs designed to support the needs for circuit awareness. The second path will be more involved with the programming of computer systems, from basic assembler, to compilers, to the operating systems needed to support new computers in the most efficient manner possible. In some cases, the two paths may be offered in two different departments within the university, the engineer through the Department of Engineering and a degree in Computer Engineering or Computer Engineering Technology, while the second may be offered through the Department of Engineering, Math, or Computer Science, awarding the degree in Computer Science.

Test Engineering

Now some might say, you almost always field-test products. Yes, very true, often where the field can be a fabric mill, a car rental counter, a hotel lobby, or a deep water oil rig. Of course, testing is not limited to the field, but may also be undertaken within a test facility within the plant. In this latter case, there will often be specialized equipment not easily transported to the field. For example in classical tests the test equipment, such as, temperature-humidity-altitude chambers, anechoic chambers, acoustic chambers, and radio field measurement chambers are all large physical units not generally portable. The point is that engineering, whatever field chosen, will probably require effort in many different environments, and involve certain sub-specialties within a given engineering field, be it civil, electrical, mechanical, or some other. One problem with test engineering is that few universities offer such a specialized degree. Test engineers generally develop through assignments in Product Test, or similar organization, where a team will perform testing on a new product to include mechanical tests, electrical tests, and software tests. In many instances, usability testing may be included to ensure the product is useable by the intended user group.

One of the authors, as an experienced cameraman, investigated a job in television, during its infancy, and was told to get an electrical engineering degree first. So, no matter what your intent is for a career, investigate the requirements, and understand the off-shoots relative to what you feel you really want to do, and in what environment, then make your decision as to any engineering field associated, if any. In this author's case, he elected to not take a TV cameraman's job, for reasons having nothing to do with the technical side, and had a very satisfying career with IBM.

From this discussion, it should be evident that the term "engineer" may encompass a variety of studies and career paths for the engineering student. It is somewhat like an onion, it appears simple on the surface, but, as you peel back the layers, there are many layers to explore. There is a growing demand in industry for trained, skilled engineers. No matter what field of engineering, engineering support, or other technical field you may choose, you must be able to communicate your findings, suggestions, or results to others. Those others will in many cases be other technical or scientific persons, and such communication may be easy. On the other hand, those others will often be non-technical persons such as business oriented management, sales people, product or service users; people who are not technically trained. It is your responsibility to make yourself understood, whether it be in writing reports and proposals, or speaking at conferences. This is one aspect of scientific and engineering fields that both authors found absolutely essential in their work as engineers, instructors, and managers. One other aspect of engineering that must be remembered is that over time the field will change as new materials, technologies, and applications are brought to the marketplace, regardless of the engineering degree obtained. As a result, you will need to maintain your skill set by continuing education and training. Find the particular subjects you best enjoy and pursue the necessary courses to fulfill your dream – and be an "Engineer".

Other Reading

Criteria for Accrediting Programs, ABET, Inc., www.abet.org.

Barger, M., Richard, G., and Snyder, M. (2010). *"Manufacturing Career Pathways"*, Manufacturing Engineering, April 2010.

Spencer, R. and Floyd, R. (2010). *"So, You Are Going To Be An Engineer?"*, IEEE Potentials, May/June 2010.

Chapter 3 – Product Development

A product's success, or failure, may often depend on how well the product was defined before it was developed. Some products based on a developer's concepts may become popular and in demand, but, in most cases, because of the narrow perspective of a developer's specific application, such products rarely hit the high revenue mark. To raise the probability of success for a newly announced product or product enhancement, both the marketing and development communities must have a road map of the direction they wish to take. These road maps are referred to as Market Requirements and Product (or Technical) Specifications, both of which are required for the Testing organization to develop a comprehensive Test Plan. The more complete and detailed these two documents are, the greater the probability that the product will succeed in the market place.

The two documents are not developed in a vacuum by each group, with Marketing (which often includes the Sales Department, those charged with the day-to-day in-the-face exposure to the customer) writing the Market Requirements and Development the Product Specifications. Marketing may ask for new, not yet invented, technology, and Development then provide a time table which is too long and too expensive. Such differences must be negotiated and resolved. Special features may require new algorithms, or other development work that will not meet the Marketing expectations – and the features may be so narrow in scope that the lack of them will not affect the overall acceptance of the product by the user community. In many cases, the Marketing and Development groups will modify and discuss both documents until a consensus can be arrived at – something to meet the market needs, in a reasonable time, at a reasonable cost, with the most highly desired features present. In addition to Marketing and Development, two other organizations are called upon to help ensure the product requested and the product delivered meet. Those two organizations are Product Test and Quality Assurance. The more specific roles carried out by Product Test and Quality Assurance will be investigated in later chapters.

A closer look at the two documents may help the reader understand the importance of each and how they relate, as well as the interactions between the groups involved in the product development.

Market Requirements

Most successful products have their success grounded in complete market research taken on *before* the product is designed. While there are a number of facets to be discussed within the Market Requirements document, perhaps first, and foremost, is "Who is the intended user group?" Immediately behind that is the question, "What problem, or problems, will the proposed product solve?" If either question is found to lack a definitive answer, perhaps the funds for the development undertaking would be better placed elsewhere. In some cases, the breadth of the possible applications may not be fully anticipated in the process of writing the Market Requirements document. Consider, for example, the simple requirements for road building equipment. Two sets of extreme conditions, personally experienced by Spencer, are real-life cases of environments in which the same kinds of equipment were required to perform similar tasks under totally opposite condition extremes. Case one was road building equipment; trucks, bulldozers and graders, etc. to build a road over forested mountains, then down through the densest jungle in the world within a war zone. There were summer monsoons of 300 to 500 inches of rain each spring-summer season, and another 100 to 200 inches during winter monsoons. Diluted fuels, rust, fungus, and so forth were daily problems that had to be overcome to accomplish the road building tasks. The other extreme was California's Death Valley that is absolutely arid, with summer temperatures in excess of 120 degrees during the day, no rain, and limited sources of water for equipment and workers, and at times, extreme dust conditions which was non-existent in the jungle situation. The intense heat coupled with the dust infiltrating equipment wear points created havoc in the road building process.

Another example could be the Market Requirements for a new

design desk top computer used by the highly experienced engineer, which could also be installed at an airport car rental counter for use by an as yet hardly computer-literate rental clerk. In this case, documentation for the system operation, if not fully specified in the Market Requirements could result in instructions with too-frequently-used technical jargon such as to be essentially not understandable for the less computer literate user. This frequently happens with material written by technical people in other countries than the customer/user.

There are a number of items the Market Requirements should address, among these being:

- Proposed user problem requiring a solution.
- Who is the targeted user community?
- What is the sophistication of the user community (neophyte, intermediate, advanced)?
- When can the product be delivered and at what cost?
- What are the required features and/or modifications?
- Who is the competition and how are they performing (in this product venue)?
- What are the sales expectations to ensure profit (high, median, and low)?
- What is the forecast of sales?
- What languages are required to support the user and field service personnel?
- Is there any special technology constraints that must be solved?
- Strengths, weakness, opportunities, and threats (SWOT) analysis for the product.
- Is there a growth path for the product and future model enhancements?
- What is the Mean Time Between Failure (MTBF) criteria expected/required?
- What is the Mean Time To Repair (MTTR) criteria expected/required?
- Are there any special or unique needs for testing by Product Test, Quality, and handling by the Field Service organization?

Note the word *required* inserted into the MTBF and MTTR list items. There is a significant difference between *expectation* and *absolute requirement*, and these differences must be understood and agreed to by Marketing and Development.

Product Specifications

Specifications are something more than simply a passing reference when talking, or learning about products and product design and development. Specifications should embody an underpinning of market requirements and existing standards, as well as use, user and maintenance requirements and limitations, as well as performance requirements.

Product Specifications and Technical Specifications are often used interchangeably, but should not be. Product Specifications will normally provide a *functional* description of the product, including such aspects as weight, size, performance, temperature (transit, storage, and operating), power, maintenance issues, interfaces, connectivity, compatibility with older systems, languages for displays and documentation, and any certifications or standards the product must adhere too. This is not a complete list, but it is important to note that none of the items listed designate the *implementation method* needed to satisfy the *function*. The implementation is left to the development group, allowing maximum freedom in the choice and also the possible use of new technology. As a simple example, consider the product specification of including a removable memory device. The implementation in the Technical Specification may map this requirement into including magnetic tape, diskette, memory stick, R/W CD, or even a USB connected external storage device. In short, the implementation method is left to the developer – as long as the implementation meets the Product Specification requirements.

One important aspect of the Product Specification, often overlooked, is that the specifications must be able to be *verified* by Product Test, Manufacturing, and Quality. For example, for the specification to state that the equipment must operate from commercial power is not verifiable. It begs the questions, "What commercial power? What voltage or voltages? What frequency? What variation is allowable? What is the maximum current load?" In each question, national and international differences must also be recognized.

The Product Specification will normally list any standards that the product will be required to meet, for example UL/CSA safety requirements. In addition, any industry standards or international standards that will be required to be met for sale of the product in countries other than the home country of the product.

As noted previously, Market Requirements and Product Specifications need to cover a wide range of product aspects, such as:
- the intended market(s),
- user description(s),
- use conditions expected to be encountered, and,
- those to address the acceptable limits:
- mean-time-to failure,
- mean-time-to-repair,
- required through-put,
- load capacity,
- temperature and humidity high and low limits,
- vibration and/or impact,
- sound/noise level limits,
- serviceability and operational access requirements, and
- all documentation to be used by the product manufacturer, intended users, and those who will service and maintain the equipment.

Not to be ignored are national standards established by and for industries, as to their products and services. Those too must be explored when developing product and services specifications, and the test plans for evaluating those.

Marketing and Development must work together in order to hope to ensure the successful introduction of new products. Either, working independently, may get lucky, but product history will demonstrate more often that is not the case. Marketing must understand the market place, the user community, and the competition. The new product requirements must be carefully thought through and documented as guidelines to the Development community. Given the requirements, it is then up to Development to determine what can and cannot be done within the confines outlined by Marketing. It is critical to get it right the first time. If there are problems, fixes can be costly, both in dollars and public image. It is also essential that tests be planned with a firm knowledge of all requirements. That can include plans for manufacturing and test abroad. Once consensus is reached, given a reasonable expectation, the product introduction should be a success.

Other Readings

Cooper, Alan (2004). *The Lunatics Are Running the Asylum*, Sams Publishing.

Floyd, R. (1988). *"Robotic Languages – Who Are The User's?"*, ASME Computers In Engineering 1988 Coference, pgs 307-311.

HIS Engineering. *Getting What You Want: How To Write a Product Specification*, www.hisengineering.com.au.

Johnson, S. (2009). *Writing the Market Requirements Document*, Pragmatic Marketing.

Shired, D. MRD – *Market Requirements Document*, www.birds-eye.net.

Chapter 4 – Product Test

Most organizations have some type of product test function. The process may be informal and accomplished by the product developers, or more formal with the implementation by an independent testing organization. In this text, the location and structure of the testing group is not covered. Rather the function and approach to testing is emphasized: the role of the product tester, the responsibilities placed on the tester and the broad skill sets needed to be successful in this role.

Usually, a reason exists for developing a new product, or modifying an existing one. The reasons vary from a newly discovered need or method to be satisfied, to a purely competitive desire to have a new or expanded feature to advertise for marketing reasons. The product may be a hardware item, software, chemical, pharmaceutical, paper or whatever. The point here is that whatever the reason, the product's purpose is to fill a need, which includes function, survival, usability and maintainability within some range of environments. The product also will be used and maintained by some range of individuals. In other words, the product needs to meet a set of requirements. From these requirements, a set of specifications should follow, which is followed by product design and build. After that, the product should have a set of test requirements followed by test procedures that are used for the actual testing. The testing to be accomplished may be conducted within a lab facility or may have the need for field testing, or test and manufacture by facilities abroad. Essentially testing should occur in three stages for new products; a test of the original Engineering model, the resultant pre-manufacturing model containing any corrections from the first phase testing, and the initial production unit again containing all corrections from phases 1 and 2. A sample of a product test plan is given in Appendix C.

For example, a set of requirements for a computer processor may contain the following generalized statements:

- Able to work in benign atmospheres;
- Able to work on board ships for collision avoidance applications in an atmosphere that tends to be corrosive, and
- Able to work in fabric mills where the atmosphere contains high concentrations of moisture from steam to keep threads pliant, as well as thread particles thrown off by high speed weaving equipment.

In the various environments , the computer needs to be readily programmed, operated, and maintained by a variety of personnel. Such personnel may have language and language skill differences, as well as general educational differences. Those differences could range from highly technical, to those for whom using a computer for a clerical function, such as checking out a rental car, is a challenge.

Those are just a few of the types of requirements that should be identified and be considered when developing specifications and product design as well as test plans and procedures for them. Too often, a product, or product redesign, concepts get specifications before use and user requirements are identified and/or defined. History is filled with products that met their specification, but failed in the market. Two examples from the automotive industry are easily brought to mind with the Ford Motor Company Edsel model, and the ahead of its time Tucker automobile. In a more technical sense, International Business Machines introduced a couple of products that did not enjoy long, successful marketing lives. The first was the P70 portable computer. It became affectionately known as the "luggable", as it outweighed most suitcases of the people traveling with it. The other was one model in an otherwise very successful product. In this case, it was the IBM System/7 Model A. The system met all of its requirements, however was not successful as it did not have sufficient processing capacity for its intended application in process control. Most products fail due to not understanding the market need the product was intended to fulfill. Thus, whenever the testing organization is presented with a product for testing, and a set of specifications to use, the first question that needs to be asked is: "What are the market and user requirements, and are they documented?"

If we consider product requirement statements and product speci-fications as defining the product, adhering strictly to those parameters as limits is bound to be inadequate for testing. These documents define a carefully prescribed product and use environment. However, that is not the real world where the product must perform. Here are just some of the realities that will inflict stress on the product, i.e. its usability and survivability:

- Production or sourced material variations that place some aspect of the product at the edge of its specification tolerance limit. What is the effect on the product if all the materials are at the same extreme of their stated tolerance? This is sometimes known as manufacturing variability.
- Marketing commitments and assurances of satisfactory use for a customer's application that compounds stresses, or pushes its limits, or where manufacturing variability could create functional, usability, or reliability and maintainability problems.
- Functional user applications beyond what are defined in the requirements.
- Environmental conditions exceeding what was defined and, therefore, specified.
- Wishful thinking by many (would like the product to be bigger, faster, cheaper, more universal in application, and so forth).

The product tester must consider those factors as well as others in planning and executing the test process and evaluation of the test results. It is paramount that not only the tester, but the product engineer, the programmer and the documenter always address the question, "What if...."!

Also, testing is more than a one shot event. Testing should occur prior to—and result in reports that support—the decision to proceed or not to proceed: before announcing a product to the market place, before entering production, and before products are initially shipped. Testing should also follow any engineering or manufacturing changes, specifically doing regression testing to ensure that the changes have not impacted the general acceptance of the product. Then again, the tester must always be looking for and considering any new information gained from customer use.

Lab Testing

To accomplish the testing required, Product Test will develop Test Plans and Test Scripts. Test plans and test scripts (also called test cases, test procedures, or simply tests) are distinctly different in terms of their meaning. The test plan is the *overview* and the test script *details the implementation.*

Test plans provide the roadmap of what testing is anticipated for the product. In writing the test plan, the engineer or programmer must have full knowledge of the requirements, specifications, and expected user community to ensure proper test coverage. The test plan does not deal in test specifics. However, the test plan does have to identify all aspects requiring testing, including regression testing needs. (The item under test is a newer version of an older product that has already undergone product testing.) In the regression test plan, the new features must be included as well as making sure that older features have not been impacted negatively in the process. Test plans will cover the logical plan for hardware, software, classical, usability, reliability, maintainability and manufacturability testing of a given product. In each major breakdown, further delineation will identify specific areas that require particular test scripts to satisfy the plan, and must also include collaboration where a product is to be manufactured and/or tested abroad. The various Test Plan components are outlined in Figure 4.1.

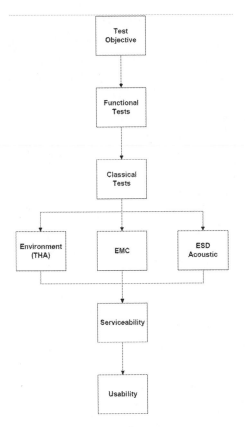

Figure 4.1 – Test Plan Components

A single test script may be sufficient to complete the required testing for a product, but that would be the rare case. Most often, many test scripts are required for each identified area of the test plan. For example, consider an arithmetic unit—how many cases are required to test addition, subtraction, multiplication, division, overflow, powers, roots and so forth A test script might use a nested routine to verify one facet, say multiplication, checking the results after each iteration. Other cases could use functions already tested; i.e., verification of powers generation could use multiplication to generate a check result.

An important aspect of test scripts frequently forgotten is that they must be documented as completely as possible. This documentation includes the function being tested, the inputs and expected results, any special requirements or supporting elements, special equipment (by type and serial number if appropriate), the test date and the results. All this information is required as "proof of performance" for final release and as support in case of a legal challenge. Frequently, test scripts are organized into libraries so various tests can use a script for testing across products. The more important reason for such archiving is for regression testing. Test scripts should be repeatable. This way they can be used to verify that pre-existing equipment performance, reliability and the like still perform against the specification as previously tested.

Beyond the functional tests, e.g. verification of feeds and speeds, correct operation and so forth, are a set of tests that require special knowledge on the part of the test engineer. These tests are referred to as classical tests: Electrostatic Discharge (ESD), Electromagnetic Interference (EMI), Radio Frequency Interference (RFI), Power Line Disturbance (PLD), Power Line Transient (PLT), Lightning Strike (LSR), Temperature-Humidity-Altitude (THA) and vibration. In some instances, for example EMI and RFI testing, there are US Federal regulations governing how equipment must perform. The tester must know these regulations, which must be considered and listed as references in the test plan and the test script. The classical tests are where testing outside the specification will most often take place. A couple of examples will help demonstrate why.

The specification for a particular product could state that input power for the product being tested is 120 volts, +/- 10%, or an input voltage ranging from 108 volts to 132 volts would be acceptable. Does that mean that the product will not operate at 107.9 volts or 132.1 volts? Probably not, and it is the role of the product test engineer to determine what is acceptable. In most cases, the input voltage will be tested to +/- 15% to +/- 20% to allow for product variability, as well as continued operation during significant power dips or surges.

In a similar manner, the operating environment for a product could state that its operational temperature boundaries are 55 to 90 degrees F, or typical office or warehouse conditions. Why then would a product test engineer place the equipment into a THA chamber and drop the temperature to −40 degrees? While the specification provides the operating temperature, it does not specify the environment the product could be exposed to; e.g., being shipped to Fairbanks, Alaska in February with the product sitting in a trailer over the weekend. In this situation, the customer does not care about shipping conditions, only that the equipment works when it is brought inside, warmed up, and turned on.

In many situations, the test activity associated with the product test can bring to light design problems which were simply not considered. Once during a vibration test, it was found that a transformer mounted at the end of a PC card had sufficient mass and momentum to set up a vibration in the board of sufficient amplitude to cause the board to snap in two. A simple restraining clamp fixed the problem. But how many boards could have been damaged during shipment if not for this simple test? More importantly, consider the impact on user acceptance, and overall market success of the new product that failed to work because of the undetected failure?

Software testing is different from hardware testing. It is more difficult to touch, feel and see! Yet, it requires the same approach for testing purposes. There must be a test plan and test scripts to document what is to be tested and how. One must consider all aspects of the software based on requirements, specifications and user expectations. Then a plan on what testing must be completed to ensure the product meets the stated objectives. In this case, the function calls, error recovery routines, interrupt routines, process control paths, outputs and file structures are all the targets of the verification process. As with hardware, software test scripts need to be defined and clearly documented for future use. They need to provide all the necessary information to define the intent of the test and the expected results. Frequently, test scripts may be combined into expanded test routines as various functions are verified and put into longer, more complex test scripts.

The most often forgotten area in software testing is in the error process. What happens when a condition fails the expected result? The product test programmer must remember to include error boundary conditions, error recovery, and even error detection so the condition cannot corrupt the system. In most of the error condition testing, the test programmer must be constantly thinking "What if?"

The hardware and software have been tested, but is that sufficient? Simply put, "*No.*" As part of the test plan, the working integration of the pieces must be verified. The *system* must function as specified. What's more, manufacturability, maintainability, usability and reliability must be addressed. For most products, it is impossible to test every combination of hardware, software, applications and operating environments that conceivably exist or occur. As a result, the product test engineer must make some educated assumptions based on stated requirements and general user knowledge. The latter can be gained through market research, surveys, or through hands-on testing by "typical" users. One important aspect of the system test is gathering the knowledge of how units and application programs interact during operation. A power supply that tested well within limits may suddenly fail because of the changing load demands, causing the power regulator to fail. Of course, finding such a failure will assist the test engineer next time: to provide a varying load during the power supply test to enable earlier detection of such problems.

Systems testing is the opportunity to test a variety of loading conditions on a given system environment or configuration. For example, in a real-time process control system, a test program could be written to verify the detection, processing, and response to closely spaced or overlapped sensor inputs. What happens when simultaneous interrupts or events occur? A key element that is also achieved during system test is in the validation of marketing claims – "The Model XYZ is 2.5 times faster than the prior version." Is this marketing hype or can such claims be substantiated by recorded results of a system test? Are there special conditions, data sets, algorithms required to achieve the 2.5 gain? With questions of truth-in-advertising and many examples of lawsuits over product claims, the importance of system testing cannot be overemphasized. Finally, it is only at the systems test level that individual products begin to overlap in timed operations, overlap in power requirements, provide loading on data buses, and the list goes on. Without the systems test, many questions must go unanswered. Without the empirical testing of the pieces as a whole, the result is mere conjecture.

More than once, we have heard the rhetorical question, "What is this saying?" when reading an operating instruction document. Often even the illustrations fail to help. The same confusion as to how to actually operate some equipment arises. Both problems too often occur because the person doing the writing, the development, or even the basic testing are evaluating usability based on their level of understanding and familiarity. For probably most products, such approaches will lead to inappropriate assessment, and a less successful product. Familiarity with the intended and actual user population—even using a cross section of them as test subjects—is essential to avoiding these usability failings. One aspect not yet discussed is frequently referred to as simply RAS. In this case, the acronym stands for reliability, availability, and serviceability. RAS can be discussed at the lowest element (power supply, diskette reader, and so forth), but most often is of greatest concern when referred at the systems level. What then is RAS?

Reliability is normally a specified criterion based on defined environmental, usage, and maintenance criteria. Since real life conformance to all of those criteria as outer limits is a rarity, stress testing beyond the limits in each area is wise. This includes testing various combinations because interaction effects most likely will occur. Reliability perception is frequently driven by user expectations. When one gets into a car and turns the ignition key, the car is expected to start. When a phone is picked up, an auditory dial tone is expected. If these events occur, reliability is the perception. Reliability then is the probability that a given product, system, network, and so forth will continue to function over time. Reliability is frequently stated in terms of mean-time-to-fail (MTTF) or mean-time-between-failure (MTBF), where the number stated is intended to assure the user of the "goodness" of the system.

System availability and reliability are frequently confused. The significant difference in the two is that reliability is a measure of the system's ability to operate, while availability is a measure of the system being available for use, even considering that it may not function correctly. As an example, a system server may have excellent availability (runs forever), but continues to have frequent data corruption (not very reliable). Availability is usually stated as a percentage (90 percent, 99 percent, 99.9 percent, etc.) and refers to the period of time a particular system is expected to be available over some arbitrary period. The arbitrary period is most often given as a year. In this definition, a system availability of 90 percent translates to a system that will be down more than thirty days in a year! If the system is suppose to provide control of a factory process, or provide interconnect service, such availability is normally unacceptable. Systems in critical applications may have availability ratings of 99.99 percent or higher. In these systems, the expectation for the system is that it will be available for its intended function with no more than a one hour period of down time on an annual basis.

Serviceability is made up of two elements: routine service comparable to a lube job on your car and problem fixing that also has two parts. They are diagnosis and repair. These areas in turn require tests that assess the adequacy of the defined routine maintenance, the problem diagnosis and repair, as well as the ease of doing each. There also needs to be testing to evaluate adequacy of diagnosis procedures, tools, procedure instructions and diagrams for all parts of the product, both hardware and software. Here again, stress tests are needed because problems are not always simple and single; one problem may, and often does, shadow another.

After prescribed testing and support for the product in model form, the manufacturability must be assured. If manufacturing has found no glitches in the design as to ability to manufacture the product, they then proceed to use their planned processes to produce one or more initial units. These units in turn must be tested against all the criteria used for the model(s). The results determine whether the production unit can be released into production. There too, does the unit function, and is it as useable and serviceable as required. The answers to these questions may, and often do, result from a field test in the live user environment(s).

Field Testing

Generally speaking, we think of testing as a laboratory exercise, a carefully controlled process. However, many products cannot be thoroughly tested solely in the structured environment and process of a laboratory procedure based evaluation. Certainly, most products require evaluation in the laboratory, at least for initial assessment and debugging. While many environments can be reasonably reproduced in the laboratory, there are environmental and physical interactions that cannot be satisfactorily reproduced artificially; they need to be found in the "real world". Hence, the very challenging and often interesting use of "Field Testing". Getting a newly developed product into field trials requires a whole separate exploration and identification of Who, What, Where, When, Why, and How of the test being planned. Careful, thorough planning is absolutely essential.

The first question the test leader must answer is whether or not the environment to be experienced for the new product evaluation can be completed in the laboratory? If the answer is "no", then consideration will need to be given to testing the product in the field, and the sort of conditions needed to complete the product evaluation and the planning required to arrange for the tests. The product technical specification and the product test plan can be used to better understand the depth of the testing required, and the tests that are required to ensure the product will operate in the intended environment. Depending on the size of the organization, the specialized test fixtures may not exist within the company, or the skills necessary for the product evaluation may also be missing. Because of such test limitations the question of "Who?" will need to be answered.

The answer to the "Who" question has a number of considerations, including cost, schedule, certified test labs, and special requirements necessary to satisfy certifying agency for the new product. Such agencies include the International Standards Organization (ISO), ASTM International (formerly American Society for Testing and Materials), Canadian Standards Association (CSA), American National Standards Institute (ANSI), and the International Electrotechnical Commission (IEC). Because of the noted considerations, it is sometimes expedient to take the product into the anticipated operating environment to test it under true field conditions – the field test.

The "What" question must look at the product specification, and most often will find limitations on internal test equipment, especially when topics such as the operating environment, i.e. weightlessness, deep sea pressures, contamination, altitude, humidity, and vibration must all be considered. The authors, during their work in Product Test, had the opportunity to test a new system to be used on-board a ship as part of an anti-collision system. In the site laboratory, they could simulate high and low temperatures, high humidity, and high altitude using a Temperature-Humidity-Altitude (THA) chamber. They could also simulate the effects of vibration in two dimensions using a shaker table, thus the effects of XY, XZ, and YZ vibration could be observed while varying the frequency and g-forces applied to the equipment. What couldn't be measured in these two tests was the effect of salt air, the massive vibrations that a ship can suffer in rough seas, the inherent vibrations caused by turning screws and wind in the rigging, and the effects of closely passing ship traffic, e.g. in the English Channel and similar shipping lanes. To gain a better appreciation of these multiple effects, a field test was conducted for a six month period – and the knowledge gained allowed the system to be modified to survive in the hostile environment and become a successful product announcement.

The answer to the question of "Where" to conduct the field trial is not always simple and straight forward. There may be a combination of requirements that need to be validated, and no single lab or field installation can provide an environment to satisfy all of them. In some cases, the site may be at a customer location. In another experience of the authors, the equipment was intended as a process control system to operate in a rug weaving mill. When the test was conducted, the impact of the weaving dust and humidity caused an accumulation of muck within the equipment dictating a complete overhaul of the filter system being used. When the possible impact to production, operator concerns, and other considerations are studied, the better the customer relationship, the better the chances for success – even if there are downturns or equipment modifications required during the evaluation. There may also be situations that require more than one field test site, simply because there are too many variables to address at a single site.

The question of "When" has been answered from one perspective, that being when particular operating specifications cannot be tested in normal lab conditions. Another facet of "When" concerns the planned announcement and ship of the new product. In this latter case, the testing needs to be late enough in the schedule to have confidence the new product meets the conditions that can be tested, but early enough that extended testing may be accomplished in the field prior to the final commitment to manufacturing, announcement, and shipment to customers. There may also be more than one field environment to be used for tests. The earlier the field test can be accomplished has one additional gain, field support personnel will have an opportunity to understand the new product before it hits the customer locations, new manuals can be verified, and any special tools obtained and used.

The "Why" has already been partially addressed. There are two simple reasons why field tests may be done (or required); 1) the product cannot be adequately laboratory tested to the environmental conditions in which it is to operate, and 2) there may be national or international standards that must be validated in operation before the equipment may be installed. Some of the standards include safety, non-interference with existing equipment, and may also include certification for insurance purposes.

The better the product specification and market requirements are understood, the better the chance for success in the new product. In some cases, the market requirements are based on the best knowledge available, but lack customer expectations because the right set of questions had not been asked. The authors were involved in a radio frequency identification (RFID) project, which appeared easy on the surface. The problem came to light when the customer, for the first time, asked "How close can vehicles be without shadowing the tag?". Great question! The only way to verify the answer was to have vehicles almost nose to tail, at 45 miles per hour, going through the various read zones to determine if there was a problem or not. Fortunately, there was no problem, and the customer was satisfied with their new system.

Such a spectrum of consideration and planning is essential in the successful development and producing a satisfactory product. Knowing that some equipment testing cannot be completed in the lab, it is essential that all of the questions be answered as fully as possible before undertaking a field test. Having said that, understand the need for field testing, and don't overlook the opportunity to develop and ship the best product possible.

Test and assurance is a demanding and complex task requiring many skills—technical and otherwise. It also requires the ability and inclination to innovate. Finally, the tester must be able to document and express him or her-self in a professional, and understandable manner. Someone else can follow what was planned, done along with the results and conclusions. What we term the "gee whiz" and "jargon" language should be ruled out of all test reporting. Remember, the test results are often the legal tie to a product being readied for release to the market. Testing is a challenging opportunity for those who wish and/or need to understand the product and its use and user environment, all in a single package. It is a career that is unique from this perspective.

Other Readings

Spencer, R. and Floyd, R. (2004). *"Product Testing"*, IEEE Potentials, April/May 2004.

Spencer, R. and Floyd, R. (2011). *"Why Field Test?"*, IEEE Potentials, Jan/Feb 2011.

Spencer, R. (1983). *"Planning, Implementation, and Control in Product Test and Assurance"*, Prentice-Hall, Inc., Upper Saddle River, NJ.

Chapter 5 – Quality Assurance

Quality is one of those funny little words that is bandied about, as in statements like, "It is a quality product...", or "She has great qualities for...", or any number of similar uses. In each instance, the speaker is attempting to identify some level of value to be placed on the object, or objects, being considered. Perhaps the biggest problem associated with such approaches is that the meaning will vary from person to person – each placing their own weight and experience onto the meaning of "quality" from their perspective.

The International Standards Organization (ISO) has placed great emphasis on what businesses need to do as part of their product development, manufacturing, and support to be rated as a "quality manufacturer" – and can be recognized as an ISO-9000 certified business, a standard to be achieved for international recognition for the business. Some requests for bids require ISO-9000 certification before the business can submit for a particular contract. In the case of ISO, they do not try to define "quality", rather they provide processes that, if followed, will lead the company to perform the various engineering, quality, manufacturing, and other functions in a quality manner. For example, are there operator procedures available? Are the procedures written in terminology understandable to the operating personnel of that system? Are the procedures up to date? Are the procedures being followed by the operator? Are the procedures updated in a controlled manner and approved by the appropriate management? None of these questions define "quality", however, given the proper procedures and approvals, they can lead to a higher quality end product.

Some Myths Concerning Quality

"Quality will be added on when the product is completed." Quality is not something that can be bolted, welded, glued, etc. onto a product when it is ready to be shipped. Quality must be designed into the product at each step of the development process. That need for quality at each step includes requirements, specifications, documentation, drawings, inspections, assembly, and test. At each step, the "quality" of the final product will be affected – for good and/or for bad. Consider first article inspections. If the parts are being brought in from a vendor, the first parts should be inspected – against the design drawings. If all the parts pass that inspection, then the vendor may be qualified to continue to supply parts for the new product. Does that mean there are no further inspections of that part? No! Periodic inspection should still be used to ensure that the parts are continuing to be to print, or the vendor may be required to certify that the parts meet the required dimensions. Possible impacts to this process could be an engineering change to the part and part drawing, or selection of a new vendor. In either case, a new first article inspection should be accomplished, once again to ensure the new parts meet specification. Also, if the print is changed, then the vendor responsible for that part must be given a copy of the affected drawing (with possible re-work or scrap charges if finished parts are already in the supply chain). Along the same line, any parts in inventory must also be reviewed against any drawing changes, or inappropriate parts may make it to the assembly process.

A couple of examples of the need for a strong quality organization and their involvement with engineering for product success in the field are appropriate. First, was in a motor fabrication process that had used the same vendor as a supplier for the copper rods used in the rotors. The vendor had been originally qualified, and had worked with Engineering over the years to come up with the final part – 99% pure copper, drawn to size according to the Engineering drawings and specifications. The part hadn't changed in years. Purchasing decided to seek a better price for the part, and moved the part order off-shore. When the new parts came in, Quality did the requisite first-article inspection, and the parts met *the existing print.* When the parts were placed into the assembly process, the copper appeared to be more like spaghetti than metal. When the problem was researched, it was discovered that the original parts had been changed from H2 hardness (soft) to H4 hardness (hard), but the drawing had never been updated. All of the changes were done *verbally*, and the documents were never updated. The failure impacted manufacturing time loss, parts scrap costs, missed customer shipments, and the additional cost of air freight of replacement parts.

In the second example, the failure was more subtle. In this case, electric motors were using oil as an internal coolant. As the motors operated to an internal temperature of 450F, the oil specification was that the oil in use had to have an operating temperature of at least 500F. Once again, in a cost cutting effort, a new vendor oil was approved and purchased for use in the motors. When motor failures began to be reported, the failure was first attributed to a failure in the motor, insulation was breaking down allowing the motor to short out. In the ongoing investigation, it was noted that all of the failing motors had a couple of problems in common; they were all operating in the 425F to 450F internal temperature region, and all were using the new vendor oil. A special set of tests were completed and the results reviewed with the vendor. As it turned out, the vendor oil blend used esters as part of the chemistry. This blend, at a temperature of approximately 425F, would decompose, allowing the esters to become isolated and attack the insulating varnish used in the motor windings. The motor oil specification was changed to not allow esters or diesters in the oil blend, the vendor changed their blend, and the motor problem was solved. In this case, Engineering and Quality should have taken a closer look at the supplier's oil, asking more appropriate questions in order to prevent the problem occurrence.

"Quality will be tested into the product." Testing will never add or subtract quality from a product. Testing can ensure that a product performs to requirements and specification, but cannot directly impact the "quality" of the product, or the perception of quality in the eyes of the users. In some companies, there is an organization known as Product Test. The function of this group is to certify that the new product meets both the Marketing Requirements and the Development Specifications. In conducting their testing, Product Test will test outside of the product specifications. For example, if the product is to operate on a operating frequency of 50-60 Hz, +/- 3 Hz, then Product Test would typically test the product from 45 to 65 Hz, allowing for part variability during production.

At one point in their careers, the authors were tasked to evaluate a number of personal computer products from several different vendors. The intent of the evaluation was to ensure that an about to be announced new product was equal to, or better, than what was available on the market at the time. While the testing did not add quality to the new product, it did introduce a number of changes and improvements to the unannounced product prior to its introduction into the market. Those changes did impact the product's success as measured by sales and customer acceptance.

"Quality is too expensive." The cost to the product to do the various quality functions is expensive, but considering the negative impacts to the product of bad parts, scrap costs, lost assembly time, and, most importantly, loss of revenue due to user returns and bad publicity, quality is a cheap form of insurance for product success. One of the most common quality problems run into today can be found in the form of a product's operating instructions that have been translated from Japanese, Chinese, Spanish, Russian, etc. into English. It doesn't matter if the product is highly technical in nature, or as simple as putting a swing set together – the nuances of the English language somehow seem to be outside the understanding of the person doing the translation. The added quality cost of having an English native speaking person review the document prior to shipment would certainly help offset the cost to the product's success in terms of the level of customer frustration and dissatisfaction the product will encounter otherwise.

The value of a Quality organization to any product cannot be over emphasized. From the inception of a product in the Market Requirements, to the Engineering Specification, vendor selection and qualification, manufacturing assembly processes, and review of customer satisfaction ratings, Quality impacts the company's success or lack thereof. It can't be added-on or tested-in, quality needs to be involved along the entire development process. Failure to do so practically ensures problems in the field – at the customer's location. You don't want problems coming from that direction, ***so fix "quality" into the product from the very beginning.***

Other Readings

Bengston, D. (2010). *"Process Measurement Is Critical"*, Manufacturing Engineering, March 2010.

Levinson, W. A. (2010). *"The US Cannot Afford Cap and Trade"*, Manufacturing Engineering, April 2010.

Chapter 6 – Human Factors

Engineers conceive, design, assess, drive production, evaluate and test, install, provide for operation and maintenance of various products. They then are responsible that those products are able to be installed, operated, and maintained by those persons responsible to perform those functions. Such persons may be installation technicians, clerks as operators, and the maintenance/service technicians, all of varied levels of skill across the total user base.

Too often, engineers, technicians, programmers, and technical writers assume that the product usage requirements are intuitively obvious to the user. Too often that is definitely not the case; hence the need for engineers concerned with those factors, who should consult on the design, or actively take part in the design, and the instructions for installation, maintenance, and operation. Those performing this function are generally referred to as Human Factor Engineers. They should be, and sometimes are, called into involvement relative to the human interface elements of the product or equipment in question, along with the associated documentation both in initial concepts and later in its evaluation, both before and after manufacture of the initial unit.

For instance, consider some of these more specific factors:

1. Reviewing design versus requirements, and working with engineering models, and later initial production to evaluate ease or difficulty of doing human required functions, and inform development and/or manufacturing engineers of what is needed for resolution of the problem(s) identified.

2. Ease of parts assembly being done by humans, and are the persons doing so able to maintain the required tolerances?

3. Ease of access to operations and service personnel for operations and servicing provided for?

4. Finally in the field of early deliveries, how well can the customer's people do the required functions and understand and use the associated documentation?

All of that requires assessing not only the hardware and software, but the documentation, any user training programs if involved, which includes training of customer operating personnel and service personnel; as well as provider's documentation and training for the service personnel.

Not infrequently, such assessment and guidance is in the hands of psychologists or engineers who have specialized in what is referred to as Human Engineering.

Spencer, one of the authors, became involved in such evaluations in one of the IBM product testing laboratories, and was called upon to work with a team of psychologists establishing a Human Factors Engineering department and laboratory within the Product Development function at one of the IBM Product Development and Manufacturing sites. Later he was involved with another psychologist for several years dealing with those who were writing product operation and training materials so both technical and non-technical people could understand manuals, and other materials written for them to use. This work involved IBM laboratory sites in the USA, Canada, and Europe.

Various Human Factor consideration examples:
- Size and/or weight of the items people, male and female, must lift and/or position.
- Height to which and/or positioning factors of items persons must lift and/or position.
- Access for any manual functions, i.e. installing, operating, or servicing, and similar considerations relative to other machines commonly in use that might be used by the same operators.
- Easily understood indication as to correctness or fault of a person's actions, i.e. materials insertion, control operated, load, position, tightening, or failure to do so, color blindness, and so forth.
- Noise levels and nature relative to nearby inter-person communication, and/or potential for hearing damage.
- Controls: the number, type user requirements, identification and associated proximity, difficulty of understanding and/or operating, access for users of various sizes, indication as to

results, color or labeling for easy identification, and relative size of the control to the size of the operator's hand.

- Appropriateness of name for the various functions.
- Care relative to color and perception by any user.
- Indication as to wrong control selection, and/or faulty choice of control.
- Care with the use of colors, ala color blindness; i.e. consider labels and/or control handles/knobs where color blindness could lead to function error, or injury of a product user, and/or servicing personnel.
- In equipment specifications, the skill and/or education levels of installers, maintenance personnel, and operators.

In establishing specifications, it is important to have available documented user requirements to indicate the personnel that will be using the product, such as:

- Installers (engineers, technicians, clerks, casual users, etc.)
- Maintenance (mechanics, technicians, engineers, clerks, etc.)
- Operators (clerks, production workers, technicians, etc.)

In other words, all aspects of human involvement must be included in design, development, production, testing, and user involvement at all levels of involved personnel. Such, in broad terms, is what we term Human Factors Engineering and assessment.

Closely associated is the need for documentation to be used by persons at each level. It cannot be assumed that the same documentation will adequately serve for persons at varied training and/or experience levels. What will be clear to an engineer or technician is not necessarily going to be understandable, and hence initially usable by the customer operators or maintenance personnel. The writer of this chapter found this to be equally true for varied documentation (user and service instructions) developed in the USA and abroad. Spencer, who is a highly experienced cameraman and photographer, bought a new camera made in Japan. He found the instruction relative to one aspect of use to be unintelligible to him. He had to consult with another user of the same brand camera to find out what was intended.

Remember one truism; both children and adults can take things apart, but not necessarily put them together again. Then too, the writer of instructions is expected to know what of he/she writes, but certainly cannot assume equal initial understandability by the reader. The writer must assume the reader needs clarity and illustration without being condescending.

Thus, the human factor applies across various areas, and the associated illustrations and instructions. It is advisable for any engineer who is responsible for new products, services, or user and service documentation to call-in and involve the experienced human factor engineers. Depending on the extent of specialization, it may be wise to call in more than one. Such involvement can save much re-do, or problem occurrence found by customers during early usage.

Remember, problems for customers of a human factors nature have a habit of being made known to many other potential users, even of being noted in a variety of journals or meetings.

This is a branch of engineering that young engineers might want to be involved in, and make a point of gaining the background for such. Spencer found it not only interesting, but of true value to the company he worked for.

Other Readings

Bridger, R. (2003). *Introduction to Ergonomics.* Taylor & Francis, New York.

Norman, D. (1988). *The Design of Everyday Things.* Basic Book, New York.

Sanders, M. and E. McCormick (1993). *Human Factors In Engineering and Design.* McGraw Hill, New York.

Spencer, R. (1983). *"Computer Usability Testing and Evaluation",* Prentice-Hall, Inc, Upper Saddle River, NJ.

Wickens, C., J. Lee, Y. Liu, and S. Gordon-Becker (2004). *Introduction to Human Factors Engineering.* Prentice Hall, Upper Saddle River, NJ.

Chapter 7 – Communications 101 – Procedures, Papers, Documents, and Reports

So often, when people are very familiar with something, there is a tendency to assume that others have a similar familiarity, which too frequently is not the case. Both of the authors have experienced this. As product test engineers, and as managers of testing departments we have run into the case of development engineers and managers who have assumed that because something in their product is not a problem to them, it therefore cannot be a problem to others. In one case, a product still undergoing development was also being demonstrated to potential customers. Whenever it was being demonstrated to a potential customer, a test engineer observed that before talking to the customer, the sales representative shut the machine off and then talked. When operating the machine, one could not carry on a conversation. The machine was too loud to be able to understand each other. When informed of this, the developing engineer shook his head and pointed to a cabinet full of patents in his name. During a meeting to discuss the testing progress the noise issue was brought up, and the developing engineer again shook his head. At that point, the testing lab manager said, "Look (----), it's too damn loud." The response was "Oh, I see, we'll fix it". They did, and that product enjoyed high success.

The point here is that as engineers it pays to listen to an assessment of your work with an open mind. Also, as the engineer making the assessment, be sure of your facts, and have the information/data to support your position. Present your information clearly and understandably to the other party. Incidentally, we are not advocating the use of profanity to make one's point. In this case, both managers knew each other very well, and respected each other as professionals. No offence was meant or taken. Such cannot be, nor should be, assumed.

One of the most often discussed topics in Human Resources meetings, and in management training sessions concern interviews and performance reviews, and the lack of communications skills in the new Associate and Baccalaureate level engineers. In most cases, the particular lack cited most frequently is in the inability of the graduate engineer to write even the most basic report. How can this be happening?

With the emphasis placed on communication skills in the criteria for accreditation of engineering and engineering technology programs, as noted in the TAC/ABET Criteria 4, Communications;

"Communications The communications content must develop the ability of graduates to:
a. plan, organize, prepare, and deliver effective technical reports in written, oral, and other formats appropriate to the discipline and goals of the program.
b. incorporate communications skills throughout the technical content of the program." (pg. 6)

It would seem continuous improvements would be noted in the abilities demonstrated by new graduates. Unfortunately, this is not necessarily the case. What then could be the problem, or is it simply a perspective of management? Is too much being expected of these recent graduates in terms of oral and written communication? Should it be the responsibility of industry to provide training in communication for their new degreed engineers?

Let us examine this topic from our perspective, or perspectives, as experienced members of industry, college professors, and, for author Floyd, a fifteen year TAC/ABET accreditation team evaluator. Having been in industry for more than fifty years, we have had the opportunity to work with, for, and have work for us a number of professional engineers and programmers. From a degree standpoint, the range would be from the Baccalaureate to the PhD, and subject matter from Mechanical Engineering, to Computer Science, to Metallurgy, and many others covering topics one would expect to find in a research, product development, and manufacturing environment. Given that large universe of engineers, we believe we would be hard pushed to identify one in four as being a good communicator, in both oral and written skills. If one were to remove those trained as technical writers, those non-native English language engineers, and some PhD people (we have wondered at times who wrote some PhD candidates dissertations), that one in four may grow to one in five or even higher.

Part of the problem can be laid in the lap of industry, as employees complete assignments, write their reports, turn them in, and they are accepted. No feedback, no re-write, nothing to help the employee understand that insure and ensure mean two different things, that it's and its are different, and that effect and affect aren't interchangeable. It could be that the supervisor doesn't know the difference, but we would rather believe they have just grown tired of trying. That is a different problem that needs addressing, but not for now. The employee needs feedback to help fill in their understanding of proper word use, grammar, and sentence structure. Without the feedback, the same mistakes, errors, and poor writing will continue – and it should not be permitted to continue. If the problem is associated with one or two members of the group, then mentoring can be used to provide the needed guidance. If it is a more general problem, it may be more appropriate to develop and complete remedial and advanced writing courses – and take the time to make sure the employees participate.

However, the problem can't be put entirely on industry, academia needs a little propping up too, as they could do more to include required communication courses, both oral and written. Having been there and done that (adjunct professors teaching graduate classes), we can see some of the practices that have been allowed to make both the professor and the student lazy, and, at the same time, detrimental to any better understanding of communication. When he entered the university engineering program, Spencer enrolled in the Writing For Engineers class. The instructor taught business letter formats and report formats as required for the student's varied class projects. There was no instruction as to easel charts for presentations, or examples of technical articles. Those things he had to learn on the job, along with the company report formatting and content requirements. For example, when was the last time a student had to write essay answers? In looking over tests from a great number of classes, we continue to see multiple choice, true/false, and fill-in the blank answer sheets for the student. We suppose the fill-in the blank could be considered a communication challenge, albeit more akin to a spelling bee. We understand that the professors are driven by less and less time to prepare classes, more students to supervise, greater pressure to publish, and continuing pressure to garner grant money for the College (all of which is part of the tenure game). Given such demands on one's time, it is easy to see that grading papers needs to be simple and done quickly. Eureka! Enter the multiple choice answer sheet with a template that can be placed over the sheet to immediately determine the grade. What could be easier or less time consuming? Unfortunately, even the grading of the papers is often done by a Graduate Assistant – who had the same communications training as the new student.

Floyd's students once called him, "Dr. Oh by the way", a name brought about through his tendency of changing the rules of projects week to week in the class. It brought the students an understanding of how things changed in the real world of products and public demands. They also were required to prepare a class project and write about their plan, what were the functions planned, how it would be implemented, tested, and released. There were no tests, lists to be memorized and spewed back on an answer sheet, not even a single true/false question. Just a term paper. Their grade was a composite, 75% based on the paper content and 25% based on grammar, spelling, and punctuation. It was tough, but he still had students that thank him for that class.

The IEEE is working hard to get better communication skills into the graduating engineer, scientist, and other people who need better reading, presentation, and writing skills. The accreditation review can help schools spot where they need more emphasis, but it shouldn't have to. Make the students read. Challenge the student with oral presentations on what they have read. Finally, make them write and then sell their propositions to their peers. Our goal should be to remove the accreditation review for communication, because Johnny can read – and write.

Reports

There obviously are many situations where within a company, management, and other internal affected groups want to know the status of a new product, or product unit that is under development, acquisition, or try-out. Possibly the most frequent type of report requested is that from the organization doing the testing.

Such reporting will usually be in one or two forms:

* Written reports

* Verbal presentations - which may embody charts, illustrations, video, or other as management requests, or which will make a report clearer, and more easily understood by individuals who are not engineers themselves.

We used to use a phrase that provided guidance to clarity and understandability: "Keep it simple".

Generally speaking, keeping it simple will be achieved by avoiding the latest "techy" catch-words and phrases. For example, programmers and product engineers seem to like to converse using their latest "gee whiz" terms, and use them in reports, documentation, etc. However, such are not necessarily understood by first time readers, users, or others. As an example, one of the authors working with a group of European engineers and programmers, who were having trouble with this concept relative to computers and programming, asked whether they expected the clerk at the airport car rental counter to understand their "gee whiz" terms. They answered "yes".

Shortly after that he slipped into use of a lot of American slang terms in presenting some information. The group stopped him and asked what he was saying. He asked if they all spoke English and they answered affirmative. He then told them he was speaking English, but with some not too commonly used American slang words and phrases. The "light bulbs" that lit over their heads were almost visible.

If it is necessary to use such less familiar words in any written text or article, have a glossary of terms and their meaning, or for reports have foot notes to clarify such terms. The point being to be certain what you say and/or write will be clear to your audience(s).

The Reporting Engineers

There are four basic groups of engineers who report or communicate in writing to each other, and to company management regards a new product.

These are Sales Engineers who should provide intended user requirements to Product Planners, the Development Engineers (includes Programming), Test Engineers, and Manufacturing Engineers (includes Quality).

Then there are the various audiences for the reporting engineers:

- Each other, among the preceding groups, which usually will be the easiest to have understanding among.
- Prospective suppliers of materials, parts, sub-assemblies, where understanding is essential for the obvious need to receive what is required.
- Responsible and/or collaborative personnel at any proposed remote test sites.
- Professional conference audiences where presentations are being made.

For all of the above, there will be varied requirements as to vocabulary, explanations, descriptions, charts, illustrations, specifications, etc. A number of these may be needed depending on what is to be accomplished as an end result of the presentation or meeting, or simply for reading by the intended audience and/or collaborators.

If there is one thing that must be understood by the writer/reporter; one size does not necessarily fit all. It is essential that the writer, and/or speaker know the intended audience/user, and their most probable level of understanding as to vocabulary/terminology. The engineer also must realize that management, and other associated project groups will want progress reporting. For instance, the author's product testing organization had what were termed A,B,& C tests. The "A" test was that of a preliminary new machine model. The "B" test was a test of the model that resulted from fixing problems reported from the "A" test, and was preliminary to releasing of the product to Manufacturing. The "C" test was of the preliminary manufactured model in order to identify any remaining problems that needed to be corrected.

Not infrequently a field test in a working/potential user site can be employed and be beneficial. For instance, the authors conducted such tests in manufacturing company plants, or an anti-grounding, anti-collision system on-board a freighter. There were many others depending on the product being developed, including one by one author coordinating testing of new products with test labs at company labs abroad.

Then also, besides the written reports for distribution to management, and other associated departments, there are verbal reports to be given to management. Those often require charts, or projected materials to support the verbal, assist in organizing presentations, and provide assistance for the audience to follow what is being presented by the presenter(s). This will generally hold true for material to be presented at professional conferences as well.

The body of the product/project report should contain the following elements:

- Title (including report level)
- Description of what is being reported; i.e. type of product and level, etc.
- Conclusion (result of activity being reported)
- More detailed description of what was done, and how, and the results of each element of the test or other type activity.
- Any backup materials, descriptions, levels of equipment used, etc.

The point being to provide that information needed by the on-going departments and personnel to do their jobs associated with the project you are doing and reporting on.

Procedures

For many years when industry was more frequently referred to as "cottage industry", there were few, if any, written process procedures for the operators. Often, the products were tools produced by the town blacksmith, or handmade furniture pieces crafted by the local cabinet maker. In most cases, the item being produced was seldom documented, even to the lack of a drawing with which the item could have been reproduced. Most of the training was accomplished through the use of apprentice programs, where young people were introduced into the trade via a long term commitment, and the trade person, i.e. the smith, carpenter, cabinet maker, baker, etc., would provide hands-on training to the aspiring young person. Each step was repeated over and over until the tradesman was satisfied that the younger person understood the process and could repeat it satisfactorily. Then, and only then, the tradesman would move on to the next task to be mastered. The training program was informal, developed by the tradesman and implemented in a step-wise process according to the demands of the master tradesman.

While time consuming and somewhat expensive, the apprentice program has continued to modern times, with programs frequently found in machinists programs (even with the advent of CNC machines), furniture making, and certain trades. Many companies have found it necessary to introduce apprentice programs into certain skill sets, as operators age and retire, leaving an opening difficult, if not impossible, to back fill. Such programs can be very expensive as it becomes an extended training program lasting several years before the new hire reaches the skill level needed. In some instances, companies have found that they require an on-going apprentice program, introducing new people as current trainees complete the program. This becomes necessary due to personnel losses through relocation, retirement, injury, or termination (even with extended agreement contracts). Apprentice programs are found more frequently in European countries, with 5 to 7 percent of the work force being involved in such training. In the United States, less than one-half of one percent of the working population is involved in apprentice programs.

In modern industry there is a much greater demand for written process procedures. The most frequent reasons include inclusion of new-hires into the production process (with limited or no training), the need to move personnel from point to point within the production area, periodic leaves, extended loss due to illness, and terminations. In each case, the person being moved may have certain requisites for the new position, i.e. mechanical tool knowledge, a general understanding of the product, test equipment knowledge, etc., but does not have the specific knowledge for the new process or product. As a result, there are few options open to the company:

1) provide in-depth training prior to the move,
2) provide an experienced operator to assist the new assignee in learning the new process,
3) provide some type of hands-on computer aided training and evaluation, and
4) provide detailed written process instructions for the operator to use.

The first option can prove to be very expensive and time consuming. With a number of products and/or processes, the cost of providing explicit training becomes prohibitive. In addition, with the mobility of trained personnel, an operator may leave upon completion of the training for self benefit elsewhere. Likewise, the second option is expensive in that it now takes two people for the single job until such time as the new person has demonstrated the requisite skills needed to produce a quality product. While the period may be measured in days, the impact to the cost to produce must be accounted for.

The third option, which will be examined in greater detail in the following paragraphs, requires support from the Information Technology (IT) group, as well as support from Engineering, Quality, Manufacturing Engineering, Product Testing, and Training, to develop, test, and implement an effective program. The object is to provide sufficient detail via a computer interface to allow the trainee to gain the knowledge necessary for success in the new responsibilities. The training program can be carried on as part of work or on an individual basis for people looking for the opportunity to advance their career. Such programs have a cost associated to them, however, the benefits of such development is the broad application to many people within the organization. Once developed, even with periodic maintenance or update cost, the return-on-investment is frequently an attractive alternative.

Computer Aided Training (CAT) has been in vogue for a number of years, and with the advent of the Personal Computer (PC), has expanded into a number of professions and work assignments. While a number of advances have enhanced the use of CAT in the training of new equipment operators or the on-going enhancement of operator skills for new programs, legal requirements, and other needs, CAT cannot replace the feel, look, and smells frequently required for complete operator activities.

CAT has a number of limitations that need to be addressed, including the need for more physical opportunities for the operator in training. For example, for the CAT program to be effective, it must be prepared by an expert at the particular process being implemented into the training regimen, and then, typically, be implemented by the Information Systems or Information Technology department, with frequent input from the Training department. Even when implemented, the program will require updates to maintain changes due to new equipment, new product, new rules and regulations, and other changes that would affect the operator's procedure. Beyond the preparation and maintenance aspects of CAT, development of testing methods must be addressed. In this case, will multiple choice questions provide sufficient evaluation of the depth of knowledge of the operator (which are easy to grade via the computer system), or will expository questions be required, or even labs to demonstrate the mastery of the operator in the new process? In the latter two instances, additional personnel must be available to review test answers and/or review lab activities to ensure the operator's knowledge.

As another major consideration, the cost of CAT must be taken into account. For a single program of training, if the cost is to be borne over a large number of operators, and the program being implemented is very stable, then the cost will most likely provide an effective solution. If, however, there are several hundred different processes and procedures that need to be taught, there are only a handful of operators to be trained, and the processes are frequently in change, then CAT will most likely not be the most effective method of training new operators.

Finally, as noted earlier, CAT cannot provide the real feel of most processes. What does it mean to tighten a connection to 1200 ft-lbs, or to measure the depth of an insert to 0.003 inches? These are physical activities that cannot be easily duplicated within the CAT system. Add to that the necessity of having to "feel" the reaction of the feed rate of material into a broaching machine, or key cutting machine, and similar devices. CAT simply cannot provide the necessary support for such training, such will involve trained operators imparting their knowledge to the student.

Written Process Procedures also requires a group for their generation. In this case, Engineering, Quality, and Manufacturing Engineering are the primary generators of the procedures. In most cases, the procedure is developed by Engineering as being the group with the most intimate knowledge of the product. Such knowledge can present problems at times, as the engineer may make assumptions about the operator's understanding and knowledge of the process, and skip over an explanation or process step essential to the successful completion of the process. Also, in some cases, the engineer will write the procedure in a single publication where, if fact, the process may encompass a number of procedures best described as multiple procedures within the single process.

Once the procedures are written, Manufacturing Engineering should become involved to ensure that the procedure clearly details the steps necessary for *any* operator to work through the process successfully. If there is doubt, or improper directions, Manufacturing Engineering must work with Engineering to update or modify the procedure. This may be a several iteration process to arrive at the final procedure, but it is a necessary process in order to make the procedures as fool proof as possible. In this development process, the Manufacturing Engineering group may also discover that certain assumptions that had been made concerning the training level of the new operator were in error, and further training is required to supplement the procedure. As an example, the new procedure may require the operator to solder pieces together, thus demanding that the operator have the necessary skill to solder correctly for this particular application (general soldering experience may not be sufficient).

Once the procedures have been written and validated, the on-going review of the procedures and their completion falls into the Quality function. Periodic reviews are needed to ensure that the procedures are being followed, that the procedures are current, and that the operator's skills are being maintained sufficiently for successful product production. Quality may also provide input to the procedures in terms of other applicable documents (such as appropriate forms), other procedures that may impact the current one, safety issues (with input from Health and Safety Engineering), and national and/or international standards to be followed.

Perhaps the most common problem with written procedures is that once they are written, other than being used by the operators, is that they are largely ignored. For example, the product may have engineering changes implemented, changes that effect the written procedures. In most cases, the operator will adapt to the new requirement readily as the old procedure was well understood, and the change is seen as something simple, merely to be accommodated in the process. Unfortunately, this totally misses the impact to the new operator, one who hasn't had the benefit of the experience of the old operator who has moved on. As a result, the new operator may miss an added step, or procedure, which doesn't show up immediately, but in the final test or, even worse, at the installation on the customer's location. In either case, the cost impact may be considerable, not even including the possible loss of confidence in the customer's eyes. Such problems could also show during an ISO audit of the company, causing a delay in certification until the problems have been corrected.

Who then is responsible to ensure that process procedures are maintained? If the engineer, test engineer, quality engineer, or manufacturing engineer were asked about their responsibilities, the answer would frequently be, "Who me?" In truth, the answer is that all four must be involved. When an engineering change is implemented, all four areas have the responsibility to review the change and understand the impacts. In particular, all four areas have to understand what, if any, changes are required to existing process procedures or the requirements for new procedures. It is important to the process that changes or new instructions be completed at the same time the change is being implemented on the manufacturing line. If not, then errors could be made in the manufacturing process, adding cost to the product.

The maintenance effort gets slightly gray when considering changing national or international standards, or the implementation of new tools on the manufacturing floor. Who bears the responsibility in these cases? In the case of changing standards, both Engineering Testing and Quality must maintain awareness of any such change, again looking at the possible impact to the process procedures. Test methods published by ASTM or API that are changed could invalidate the company's product unless the changes are accounted for in design and manufacturability.

In a similar manner, if new tools are being introduced onto the manufacturing floor, Manufacturing Engineer bears the responsibility of ensuring that the tools are documented properly and that operators are trained in the new tool use – and that procedures using the old tools are updated at the same time the new tools are introduced. It is also important that the tools meet all of the standards called for in the procedures.

Once a process procedure is written and released, it should be periodically reviewed for currency – both to the product and to applicable standards. Too frequently, the procedure is written, released, and then ignored until some catastrophe occurs – and a major cost impact has to be borne by the company. Part of the maintenance activities should be a scheduled review, much like the on-going calibration of test tools and special manufacturing tools such as gages. If during the scheduled review it is noted that the procedure requires updating, it can be routed to the responsible areas for update and re-release. It may also be found that a change may impact other documents and procedures as well, resulting in a cascade of changes that are required.

The major problems in written procedures are; 1) completeness and accuracy of the procedure, 2) maintenance of the procedure caused by changes in product or standards, and 3) being written to the appropriate language and skill set of the intended user. While the first problem can be largely overcome by having a number of organizations as part of the review process to ensure that the documents are complete, the others continue to be a major concern in industry. While engineering changes and their effect on the procedures are reasonably easy to detect, changing standards can constitute a major challenge to a company. There is seldom one organization assigned to maintain standards, much less maintain awareness of any such change's impact to process procedures. Add to that the cost of maintaining sets of standards within the corporate library, and the solution becomes even more difficult. Writing procedures and then maintaining them will consume resources from a number of organizations within the corporation, however, failure to do both can impose a major hit to the success of the company in today's markets.

Documents

The success or failure of a manufacturing company depends on its product documentation – its correctness and availability. In the first instance, information collection, document formats, and revision control are important aspects to ensure the correctness of the information available. In the second case, the effective distribution of the information across an international user base as quickly as possible is critical to a successful manufacturing process.

Over time, most companies will develop the necessary documentation to allow them to produce their products in a reasonably consistent manner. Over a several year period, one company the authors worked with developed a set of more than 7,000 drawings, with about 80% of them having been converted to CAD, the remaining being pen-and-ink drawings that had not changed for a number of years. A complete paper library was being maintained, including an archive section of all obsolete drawings. The archive allowed research on engineering changes for any particular part. Storage for this mass of drawings amounted to 24 4-drawer filing cabinets.

If an engineer required a drawing to implement a change, they would have to request a copy from the Document Control clerk, who would make a photocopy and give to them. The master copy of the drawing would then be returned to the filing cabinet. In a similar manner, if someone from Manufacturing, Purchasing, or a remote location needed a copy, it would be requested from the Document Control clerk. In the case of remote location requests, the copy would be mailed, transmitted by computer, or sent via commercial carrier overnight depending on the urgency of the request. Processing document copy requests required a dedicated, full-time clerk.

Material specifications were included on individual part drawings. As a result, if 100 parts were made of 99.99% pure copper, then the material specifications, including pertinent ASTM or other standard organizations specifications, would be listed on each drawing. There was no cross reference to the material use. As a result, if a material, or organizational specification changed, all related drawings had to be changed at the same time – and experience shows the chances were good that some would be missed.

Over the years, vendor relationships had been established such that equipment specifications were not needed. Sketches, rough drawings, and early releases were sufficient to develop prototypes for test and evaluation. In such an evolutionary approach, new products could be developed and released into Manufacturing, with new procedures re-leased to describe how to assemble and test the new product. Engineering product specifications simply did not exist. This lack of specifications put a serious roadblock in the path of Quality, as the only inspection criteria that could be used was for material or dimensional correctness – not a question of form, fit, function, or standard.

A formal Engineering Change Notice system had been in place for a number of years. Local filing for approximately three years of changes was provided, with movement to off-site storage beyond that. As in other legacy data, these files were maintained in order to access change history for any question that might arise. These files also had all support material that might have been included in the process of implementing the requested change. Multiple copies of all change notices had to be made and distributed, via mail service, to all off-site locations, including many overseas. Problems could, and did, arise from time to time, as changes were proposed and implemented, and then found to conflict with some local country or customer requirement.

In 2001, a couple of occurrences forced a look into the current mode of operation; 1) a move into a new facility with limited space, and 2) a down-turn in the economy which called into question staffing needs.

The net of the review indicated a revolutionary approach was available, if the user community would buy into it. The first step was to work with the Information Systems (IS) department to understand their work effort to establish a secure corporate intranet web site, with all locations having access to the site. Once that agreement was established with IS to support the web site, the effort turned to Manufacturing to convince them of the benefits of going to a web-based source of information rather than the old paper approach. With some initial reluctance, as most will resist change, Manufacturing agreed to try the new approach. Agreements and plans in place, Document Control moved into the implementation process.

Like many projects, it would have been nice to quit on a Friday afternoon and come in Monday morning with all the new approaches in place and working as expected. Unfortunately, few projects have such luxury. In this particular case, the priority needs had to be decided in order to meet the day-to-day operation. The order arrived at was:

- web site organization and content
- drawings
- specifications
- Engineering Change Notices (ECN)
- Other publications

Before any work was started on the web page content, the format of the data planned for the web had to be established. The plan was to provide as much information, with some security in place, as needed for remote sites to have useful information for their operations. Since document control remained a key requirement, distribution in the native formats, e.g., CAD, Word, and so forth, was not an acceptable solution. The solution was to use Adobe⁚ document formatted files (commonly referred to as PDF [.pdf] files) as being the best answer due to the ready availability of file reader software (free downloads from the web). Having made that decision, it was time to lay out the Engineering web site.

The intent was to allow the various areas to share information between them and make it available for employees use also. As a result, Engineering was given an on-line folder, ENGINEERING, into which they would place the information they wished to make available. From the corporate perspective, anyone who could successfully log onto the internet site had access to the ENGINEERING folder content. While that was acceptable for some of the planned content, it was not for everything being placed onto the site. As a result, a number of folders were established, with varying levels of permission requirements for access. Because of the nature of the publications and desired broad distribution, the following publication types were given the same access level as the base folder, e.g., once signed in, anyone could access the sub-folder.

- Application Briefs
- Field Service Briefs
- Manufacturing Briefs
- Manuals
- Software
- Forms
- Training

A second set of information required a more restricted access, from an intellectual property perspective, including the following:

- Product Drawings
- Product Specifications
- Material Specifications
- Engineering Change Notices

Once the file structure and permissions were set, the system was ready to begin to convert and populate the files with the information – and make it available around the world.

In keeping with the practice of archiving obsolete drawings and the wish to remove the file drawers jammed with the 40,000 plus "old" drawings, it was decided to purchase a document scanner. The obsolete drawings were scanned, one at a time, archiving them by drawing number into an archive folder. This process was followed for both CAD and non-CAD drawings. A new Document Control practice was written to ensure archiving of new releases automatically, so the scanning would not have to continue in the future.

A general ECN was written to allow conversion of existing CAD drawings into the correct formats, title blocks, change history control blocks, and to remove all material specification references. In the latter case, the material specifications would be replaced with a reference to a Material Specification number. As each drawing was updated, with no form, fit, or functional changes, the CAD version was returned to the drawing library, a copy placed into the archive, and a .pdf version placed onto the web site. Drawings that were currently in an ECN change process followed the same rule as part of the release process.

The non-CAD drawings went through another iteration to determine those requiring conversion to CAD, those which could be simply scanned for web display purposes, and those that could be scanned for archiving only – truly obsolete drawings. One criteria that would move a drawing into the CAD group was if there was a material specification on the drawing (other than obsolete drawings). As before, each drafter was given a folder with drawings requiring conversion and the process worked its way through until all drawings had been converted and made ready for web use. At that point, the switch from paper to paperless was ready to be thrown. As part of the preparation for the move to web access, terminals and printers had been placed in strategic areas on the Manufacturing floor and in other areas that typically required access to drawings. From the time the switch was thrown, in a period of two weeks the workload of supplying paper drawings was reduced to the level of releasing one full time clerk for other work.

One aspect of drawing control that was initially overlooked was when a drawing was entered into the ECN process. When the clerk was involved, the current drawing would be stamped ECN IN PROGRESS in order to inform anyone requesting it that a change was in progress. Thus, if the drawing was for Manufacturing or for a vendor quotation, the engineer could be consulted about the nature of the change and its effect on the product or assembly. In the new process a similar operation had to be developed. When a drawing was removed from the CAD library, a dummy .pdf file was written onto the web site, directing the requester to contact Document Control for that drawing, thus creating the effect of an ECN IN PROGRESS stamp.

As drawings were being updated and modified by the removal of references to materials, a list of newly required Material Specifications had to be developed. In addition, a standard format for both Material Specifications and Engineering Specifications had to be developed and documented for future reference. The standards were written as Document Control practices, and provided for standard content and sequence of information within the two types of specifications.

As the specifications were written and made ready for release, each was reviewed by the responsible engineer to ensure it met the original intent included on the drawing. After the engineer had signed off, the specification was reviewed by their manager and the Vice President of Engineering. At that point, a .pdf file was made and placed on the web in an ENGINEERING/SPECIFICATIONS folder. This folder could be accessed, with appropriate permissions, by the user community.

One immediate impact of this approach was in the situation of a materials change for a particular product. A search against the parts number data base for WHERE USED for a particular Material Specification would reveal all parts that referenced that particular document. In this manner, all drawings affected by the change were identified for update. A secondary benefit was if a referenced industry standard changed, i.e., IEEE, ASTM, ANSI, etc., only the Material Specification required changing, not the drawings.

Material Specifications accounted for approximately 300 documents placed on the Engineering web site. There were approximately 30 Engineering Specifications on the web, most frequently used by Purchasing for vendor quotation. Engineering Specifications were also developed using a fixed format for standardization, and follow the same sign-off process prior to release. Any proposed change to either type specification falls under ECN control.

In the original plan, Engineering Change Notices (ECNs) were not included as part of the web site content. Originally, an ECN query capability was planned, to be able to check the status of a particular ECN, but that was all that was intended. Having the new scanner, it was used to scan the backlog of ECNs in the file cabinets, placing them into an archive folder for handy reference by Document Control and Engineering personnel, and deleting the paper copy. Such an approach provided some eight years of ECN activity readily available for access on-line.

One long term problem in the paper system was in the cost and delays associated with the distribution of ECNs to other locations. In some instances, this could mean more than a week before an ECN would arrive at the destination, during which time the ECN could have been implemented and released. On occasion, it would be discovered that the ECN could not be implemented in the proposed fashion without impacting some processes at the remote location, and the implementation would have to be changed (or deleted). A better approach was needed.

ECNs were being written, reviewed, and processed on a daily basis.

As each was processed, part of the process included scanning the ECN for archiving. A decision was made to include the generation of a .pdf file, which was then placed on the web site. This provided same day release of the ECN information, allowing for immediate feedback if any problems were noted. As part of the process, when an ECN was ready to close, the closing information was also displayed on the web to allow users to understand what had been done to complete the ECN activity. Again, this allowed the users an opportunity to understand the change and its impact to their processes.

Initially during the ECN scan process, it did not include any of the attachments for archival purposes. Copies of the drawings were archived as part of the release cycle, so were thought to not be necessary. As part of the release, when the engineer agreed to the change, their signature was placed on the drawing. The drafter would convert the signature into a set of initials on the change control block, documenting the acceptance. It was pointed out that the initials did not carry the same weight of evidence as the original signature. so the process was changed to include the scanning of the signed documents for archive.

While preparing the other publications for the web, it was decided to take advantage of the web's capability for easy distribution of other information. A number of short papers, or briefs, were developed and placed on the web site. One, Application Briefs, was oriented to Application Engineers, with explanations to help them understand equipment capabilities and limitations, new product offerings, and similar topics. A second, Field Service Briefs, was oriented to field support personnel, with brief descriptions on equipment setup, installation tips, and other equipment specific instructions. There were also a number of application programs and coefficients for other programs that needed periodic update and distribution. Again, the flexibility of the web site made it easy to provide the new updates in a folder from which the users could download the updates for their local use.

The initial effort involved getting English only material published onto the web site. Over a period of time it was learned that one or two countries were converting English drawings and text to Spanish for use locally. The primary problem with such an effort was that it exposed the company to a citation from ISO as not having the base design documents under control. With the drawings being re-drawn to include metric dimensions, and texts being re-written into Spanish, two basic types of design documents had the possibility of being incorrect, out of date, or in conflict.

A conversion process was begun immediately on the drawings to include dual dimensions (English and metric) and releasing them to the web. A local vendor was also contracted to begin translating the various documents on the web site into Spanish. Two folders were established under each category of document, providing the user with a choice of English or Spanish.

With all the good aspects of the web for document distribution, what could be the downside? Let us explore that aspect using the following four views:

- exposure
- evaluation
- evolution
- expectations

For years drawings and other documents had limited distribution. Typically engineers, assembly operators, purchasing agents, and vendors were the only people with access to such documents. In most cases, even that access was limited to the immediate need of the individual making the request. Once the documents were on the web, the *exposure* mushroomed not only in the number of people having access, but the number of associated documents that could be accessed freely. Where in the past people asked for only certain documents due to the time and trouble of gaining them, the web made it easy and the demand for documents increased significantly.

As more people made use of the web and the accessibility of the documentation, they began to *evaluate* what was available. Questions as to format, content, completeness, correctness, applicability, and so forth began to filter into Document Control. In many cases the questions required only simple answers, but, in some cases, the answer meant research and considerable work to provide the answer and correct the document accordingly. While some questions were simple, each required time to research, time to process and respond.

The web is not a static entity, it is ever changing, *evolving* as the needs and uses dictate. Our experience has shown that to be true. Each time the "final" version was reached on the web site content, another idea or application would be brought forth. The addition of other language publications was not originally planned, but evolved because of a need by the using community. Being new to the use of the web, the expectation was that continuing evolution in the content of the web site would be dictated as the needs and uses of those being supported required.

Finally, once users gain comfort and satisfaction with the information being provided, the level of *expectation* rises. It seems to be a quirk of human nature, given a little information they want more. Given more, then even more is wanted – and sometimes demanded. One of the tricks is to understand what information is truly needed, so it can be supplied, and what would be nice to know. In the second case, it can be filed on that long list of evolutionary topics that may be included in some future release.

Exposure, evaluation, evolution, and expectations. All four will be experienced as the user community becomes more familiar and comfortable with the web content. It also means that the workload to support the various inquiries, additions, and changes will impact the overall workload of the department. Where the web has simplified document distribution, it has driven the system to provide more complete and near real-time answers.

Knowing what we know today, would we recommend a similar solution for other users? The simple answer is yes. The benefits experienced are many, including:

- better standards control
- more complete specifications
- up to date specifications
- quicker response to problems
- better understanding of user community
- far less paper
- superior archival system.

Any one of the benefits listed would justify the move to the web for document distribution. Taken in total, the benefits far out-weigh any detrimental effects. The greatest cause for concern was on protection of intellectual property, however, with standard firewalls for secure sites and individual file permissions, this too has a reasonable level of expectation of success.

Presentations

Your boss stops at your desk and informs you, "Tomorrow afternoon I want you to present to the Executive Staff and a couple of our influential customers a status report on Project X. You will have 15 minutes for your presentation, with 5 minutes for questions." Your first reaction may be one of disbelief – followed quickly by panic as the truth sets in. Me? An executive and customer presentation? Tomorrow? Recognize that you are not alone in your initial reactions, but you have to come to grips quickly, there is very little time to waste before your time arrives. With a few simple guidelines, your presentation can be a total success.

To begin, you need to determine the media available to you (in the conference room being used). In most cases, there will be a presentation system, including a PC or PC connection, which will allow you to use commercial presentation software packages similar to Power Point* or some other package. Given the decision to use a computer based presentation method, rather than poster board, how many slides are needed? A good rule of thumb is one minute per slide, thus 12 to 15 slides will be your limit. The actual number will be determined by the slide content and the words that accommodate each.

The next step is to develop an outline of your presentation. What information is important to your audience? In most cases, the information needed includes:

(1) brief description of the project or product,
(2) planned schedule,
(3) proposed cost of the project,
(4) current status,
(5) final projected cost, and
(6) expected projection completion date.

Note, including a title slide, the slide count is already at 7 slides. As the project description slide will probably be more than a single slide, as will the expected completion date (to describe the major steps to completion), you are in the 10 slide region. This leaves a couple spares which can be inserted, or added, based on you presentation development.

One of the most common mistakes made in a slide presentation is in crowding the slide with line after line, paragraph after paragraph, in an attempt to put all of your project knowledge before your audience. Don't do it! Limit each slide to key words or lines, and then stop. Each slide should have no more than 5 or 6 lines of information. Figure 1 illustrates a typical slide that requires a magnification glass to read – avoid such clutter! If a topic, from your outline, requires more, move to a second or third slide, always maintaining balance between the slides.

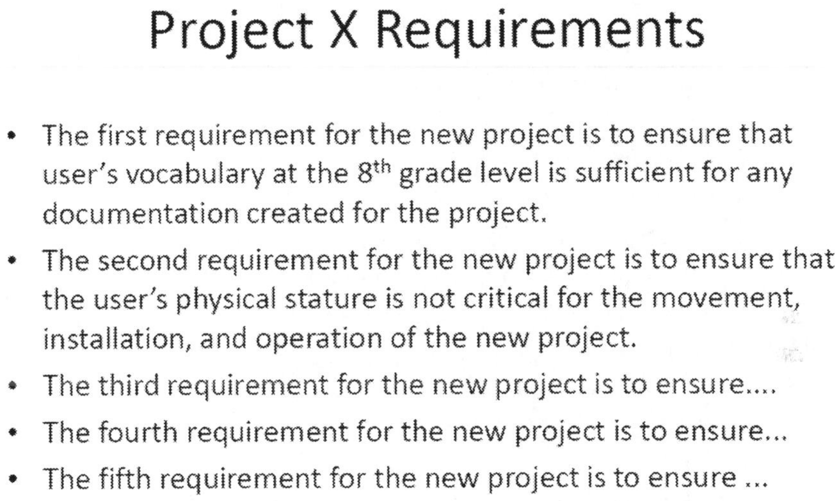

Project X Requirements

- The first requirement for the new project is to ensure that user's vocabulary at the 8th grade level is sufficient for any documentation created for the project.
- The second requirement for the new project is to ensure that the user's physical stature is not critical for the movement, installation, and operation of the new project.
- The third requirement for the new project is to ensure....
- The fourth requirement for the new project is to ensure...
- The fifth requirement for the new project is to ensure ...

Figure 1 – Too Much Information on a Presentation Single Slide

As you begin to develop your presentation, check with other engineers to see if there is some standard format used by the company. You might also check with the Marketing Department if the Engineering group has no suggestions. Try to refrain from motion type slides, or slides which change highlight levels as you make your presentation. Remember, the presentation is tomorrow, thus limiting your time to practice and correct errors. Finally, be cautious in your use of color. Avoid red and green as they typically are used in connection with loss and gain, stop and go, or danger and safe. Depending on your audience, there may be other colors that have subtle nuances for the attendees. Take time to remove any colors that might prove detrimental to your message.

You have an outline of your presentation, use it. While your slides are limited to a few key words or lines, there is no such limit on your outline sheets. Put the words you wish to be used in expanding your slide content on the outline. The outline can be placed on the lectern for easy reference. If you prepare your outline using a font type size of

14 or 16, bold print, and tripled spaced, you will find it easy to reference and follow – even as you remember to address your audience.

There are some Do's and Don'ts that the presenting engineer needs to keep in mind.

Some DO'S:
- Identify your topic.
- Keep charts or videos simple.
- Speak up clearly.
- Use terminology suitable for your audience.
- Watch for questions.
- Stay alert for questions
- Relax, you are the subject matter expert

Some Don'ts:
- Do not speak at "machine gun" rate, or with undo hesitation.
- Don't try to impress your audience with needless technical terms.
- Do not talk down to your audience.
- Don't simply read from charts or projection screen.
- Do not have your back to your audience. At most you should only need a quick glance at your chart/video screen.

One point of concern is whether you pass out copies of your presentation at the beginning or the conclusion of your presentation. There are no fixed rules, the choice is typically yours. If the slides are passed out at the beginning, the audience can jot notes on the prints for later reference. The downside is that someone may read ahead, raising questions about some later slide. In most cases, if this happens, recognize the importance of the question and note that you will cover it in due time.

Papers

Have you ever had the misfortune to attend a conference, or read a report, and after a short while asked yourself, "What was the topic being presented or discussed?" You may have wondered if a dictionary or thesaurus would have helped to decipher what was being presented. Most likely, it's not a case of ignorance on your part, rather a case of the presenter trying to impress the audience with his or her expertise, the effect can be negative. Unfortunately, while the speaker or writer may be a subject matter expert and had worked diligently on the presentation, if the audience failed to understand the points being presented, the content will be lost and ineffective. Plung and Montgomery noted, "The professional communicator, in particular, who does not consider the needs and interests of a real audience is creating a self-induced fiction. While such fiction may be sustainable through academic dialogue in the composition or literature class, it is totally inappropriate when dealing with professional communication." One important note – the term *presentation* used here refers both to written and oral presentations, as both too frequently suffer from techno-babble.

Often the speaker, or writer, may be an engineer or programmer embarking on new technology products, or new applications of an existing technology, or simply some new design features for an existing product. The question to be asked and answered before preparing the talk or writing needs to be, "Who is the intended audience?" In their years together at IBM, the authors were involved in many usability tests on new products. Most of the material was required to be written to the level of an 8th grade vocabulary, and at times even that proved to be a problem. As it turned out, not only was the educational level important, the background of the people participating in the test could influence the acceptance or rejection, of the new product. In the case of a new product having a keyboard for data entry, the authors found a number of people did not want to complete the data entry by pressing the "Execute" key - since changed to the Enter key so widely found on PC keyboards today. The feelings of the test subjects were not considered in the initial design, but the results have had a long term impact. In this case, it was not long or unfamiliar words that caused the problem, but the perception of the users that was missed in the original design.

As engineers, with many years engaged in testing products, some with new technology or programming, we were faced with describing test results or problems to the responsible development groups and various levels of management. In many cases, such reports included written reports to be read by upper corporate management with little or no opportunity to discuss the content. What was being reported had to be clear and informative to that audience, from the engineer or programmer to senior management. As noted by Harty, "The sharing of knowledge is not simply seeing facts, but rather interpreting them, and that interpretation varies depending upon one's vantage point. Communication, then, is not just shared information, it is shared interpretation....If sender and receiver are from different corporate subcultures, then achieving shared interpretation is more difficult." A specific and rather understandable example of where clarity is essential was undertaken by Spencer's father, an engineer, as he was called upon by the courts as an expert witness, a subject-matter-expert on a number of occasions. Considering that both the judge and most members of the jury were certainly non-technical people, the need for clarity and understandability in reports that may become part of a legal review is absolutely essential. In this case, Spencer's father had to be able to interpret the content of the reports, letters, or situation event causes, and explain the technical concepts to a non-technical audience in words they could understand. Stop and think. How often have you been faced with a product user's guide or manual for a new technology product such as a camera or computer, where various references to controls, inadequate illustrations, and a less than clear language seem "Greek" to you. One problem with user's guides is that they are often written originally in a foreign language, and then translated into English (or other target language). Unfortunately, many times the translations are literal from the original language, and the structure and word selection are inappropriate or incorrect in the target language.

In a study conducted by Dr. Daniel Oppenheimer of Princeton, it was found that greater use of long words, needlessly, confused the readers and the writers were judged to be less intelligent. According to Dr. Oppenheimer, "Anything that makes a text hard to read and understand, such as unnecessarily long words or complicated fonts, will lower the reader's evaluations of the text and its author." The key word here is *needlessly*, which does not preclude a long word which explicitly applies to the point at hand. Reep offers the following bit of advice; "In writing, use vocabulary that your readers understand. Defining a word with other words that are equally specialized will frustrate your readers; no one wants to consult a dictionary to understand an explanation that was suppose to make referring to a dictionary unnecessary."

When you are given the opportunity to speak or write about a particular project, take on the job with enthusiasm. During the preparation use words you are comfortable with. If the word you use just doesn't seem to quite fit the bill, or is not as concise as you would like, then, and only then, pick up your thesaurus to find the *exact* word you need – not necessarily the longest word. You will find you will be successful and appreciated by your audience. If you need to use some newly coined technical word or phrase, be sure to explain it in clear wording.

Remote Collaboration

There are few businesses today that perform 100% of their product build in-house. Most businesses will use vendors for parts production, specialty companies for sub-assembly work and test, doing only final assembly and test in-house. Additionally, some companies may have multiple facilities where production at any single facility forms only one or two sub-assemblies for the final assembly plant, which is frequently the case both in the USA and foreign sites. In any case, the coordination of the work efforts, maintenance of production schedules, cost control, and other areas of concern require close collaboration to ensure success. Typically prepared by the Engineering function, product requirements require input from Marketing to identify anticipated user needs, work force characteristics, any foreign language needs, disabled worker needs, and so forth. In addition, other inputs from Quality, Safety, and Field Service may be needed to fully define the product requirements totally.

Historically, products from a single manufacturer were common, with all of the constituent components being produced either within a single facility, or within a number of facilities – all owned by the same parent company. For example, in a furniture company, most of the parts to be fitted together to form the particular item of furniture would be produced in a single plant. This included the preparation of the lumber, cutting or machining the pieces, joining the parts together, and, finally, finishing the particular product. Common parts such as screws, nuts and bolts, and glue were typically purchased, but the forming of springs and cushions as well as the sawing of the lumber itself was probably done within the home company. Another example would be in a chip manufacturer such as IBM and Texas Instruments. The processes here include starting from the growth of a silicon ingot, started from a small seed of silicon, growing from the small seed to an ingot several inches in diameter and up to 24 inches in length. The ingot is then sliced into wafers, polished, litho-photography patterns applied layer after layer, the chips sliced into individual pieces, the chips tested, and finally mounted onto the package for assembly into various computer applications. Again, from the ingot growth to the final package, all the processes are done in the home plant.

Such approaches have changed over the years, as the cost of maintaining specialized skills, equipment, and processes have dictated a new approach. Manufacturers now typically perform final assembly and test within the home plant, however, many of the assemblies and sub-assemblies may be built, machined, or otherwise assembled by a variety of specialists or outside vendors, some out of country. This approach has placed a more severe burden on the manufacturer of the end product, as the parts must be more explicitly defined for the outside vendor and in-house quality control.

For product success, especially when diverse locations are part of the overall product development, a complete product specification is necessary. The specification provides the intended function of the product, and can also form the basis for test and evaluation of the product when finally assembled. Some refer to the specification as "feeds and speeds", details answering such questions as; power and frequency ranges, operating and storage temperatures, paint colors and types, dimensions and weights, operating speeds, current loads, limitations or exclusions, reference standards, material requirements and specifications, warnings and cautions, and so forth. It is an extensive list and takes time to prepare in sufficient detail, but it is necessary for product success. Typically prepared by the Engineering function, it requires input from Marketing, Quality, Field Service, and Manufacturing. Where multiple locations and/or vendors are involved, such specificity is absolutely required, otherwise there is an excellent chance that the parts that are delivered won't function in the manner expected.

There are two items in the list that are frequently overlooked, reference standards and material specifications. Most professional organizations have published standards for a variety of product aspects. For example, ANSI, API, ASTM, IEEE, ISO, UL and others have specific standards that affect operation, maintenance, testing, safety, and other specifics that products must meet – if they are to be acceptable in public use. Unfortunately, there are few formal specifications that can be used as references when "User Requirements" are to be considered, so the preparers of the product specification must determine those needs. For example, the authors had the opportunity to work with a new product, which was to be used in a "typical" office environment. When the sales force attempted to describe the product, the product had to be turned off – it was too loud to be heard over. A simple heavy plastic cover easily opened and closed around the offending area corrected the problem, but it was not a welcome start for the product. Similarly, foreign language documents must be phrased correctly to ensure there is no operator misunderstanding or other problems that could cause ineffective or unsafe operations by the operator.

It takes a considerable effort to maintain a current library of all of the standards that effect a product, or product set, but it is necessary if the manufacturer wishes to market to certain countries or international areas. Material Specifications are more specific, where one specification must be written for each material being used. For example, if panels on a product can be made from sheet metal or aluminum, two Material Specifications will be required, one for the sheet metal (steel type, gauge, finish, chemical content, any special requirements, what national standards must the steel meet, and any special requirements placed on the material supplier), and one for the aluminum (with similar requirements). While such careful documentation may seem more than required, it provides more insurance that the product will be built correctly, even if different vendors are brought into the process – the new vendors will provide the same material for their particular assembly or sub-assembly.

Specifications and Material Specifications will require update from time to time, due to changes in standards, functional requirements, engineering changes, and industry material changes. The new specifications should indicate the revision of the document, and whatever is used for change control noted on the cover page (along with the date of the change and any approvals required). Such updated documents should be distributed to all affected parties so everyone involved is working with the most current documents.

Where the specification provides the expected functional description for the product, it is the drawings that provide the guidelines for the production of the parts. In modern plants, product drawings will normally be in two dimensions, using CAD application software, or three dimensions, using SolidWorks or some similar software application. Whichever type of drawing is used is not critical, but the requirement for the drawing is. Included on the drawing should be both English and Metric values for all dimensions. On the discussion of dimensions, care should be used to not over-specify dimensions. Each digit added to the tolerance increases the cost of the part and, consequently, the cost of the product to produce. The difference between a dimension of 3.0 inches and 3.000 can increase the cost of a part by up to 15 times. That is not to say that 3.000 is not correct, if it is a critical fit dimension that must be maintained. Unfortunately, too many engineers over-specify the tolerances, believing it is necessary – when it isn't.

Another important item concerning drawings is in maintaining revision control when changes to the part, or assembly, occur. Parts cost can quickly climb if the vendor is working with Revision B and the part has been modified (on paper) to Revision C. The part will either have to be scrapped entirely or reworked, at additional cost, before it can be used. It is the responsibility of Engineering to ensure that all users of the drawings have the most recent version. As revisions are made to drawings, archival copies should be kept to provide change tracking and verification if a particular change requires deletion or replacement.

Also, some type of change control should be implemented on the drawings. While Engineering is responsible for change implementation, other areas such as Quality, Safety, and Manufacturing Engineering should review proposed changes so they can understand the impacts to the various processes and procedures in use within the manufacturing process. All changes should also be listed on the drawing, at least in some short description, again allowing easy tracking of changes and when they were implemented.

One aspect frequently overlooked is drawing ownership. Who owns the rights to the drawings? This is a decision that must be made at the beginning of a project or product development. If the part, and its drawings, is designed, built, and sold by the vendor as a standard part, such as a temperature transducer, then the drawings would normally remain the property of the vendor. On the other hand, if a part is being manufactured as part of a development contract or purchase order, then the drawing should belong to the product manufacturer. This ownership needs to be established during initial contract negotiations. Another point on ownership is that all drawings should carry the logo of the parent company, as well as a note concerning the confidentiality of the drawing.

Finally, where established, the Material Specification, or specifications where more than one material is noted, should be identified on the drawing. This allows vendors, or others, to ensure that the materials being used in the assembly or sub-assembly are correct.

Increasingly, organizations are geographically distributed with activities coordinated and integrated through the use of information technology. Software is frequently outsourced by the parent company, unless there are specific trade secret concerns with the particular application. Sometimes there may be a qualified engineer who can do the necessary programming, but that is infrequently the case. Most times the development effort will have to be subcontracted, or, perhaps, written by the IS or IT department, depending on the skills and workload of this alternate group.

Much like using a vendor to produce parts to drawing specifications, the software development effort requires specific details to be used by the contract developer. Note the word contract. That implies a specific schedule, delivery items, and costs to be incurred. Unfortunately, too often a program development effort is undertaken before the program specifications have been written, reviewed, and agreed upon. As a result, frequent changes are introduced during the development process, causing massive overruns, cost, and delays in delivery. It is a bit like saying, "I need a program to test my new product." That sounds like a program that will cost tens of thousands of dollars and never be delivered – there is nothing specific to be delivered, so how can you tell if you are finished?

Another issue with contract software development is who is the owner of the final product? Too frequently this question is ignored, or overlooked, until the application is delivered – in executable form. There might be a User's Guide of Operation, but nothing else. When changes have to be made – and they will – a new contract with the same vendor will be required, as the source code remained with the vendor. Thus, even after paying for the development, the contracting company is held ransom for any changes or enhancements to a program they have already paid for! Make sure the deliverables include user's guides, executable code, and the source code. In this manner, the contracting company may use the same vendor or look elsewhere if they wish. Finally, the test and evaluation personnel need to assure that all documentation for customer use will be understandable by the intended users.

A software application requires a specification just like an engineering specification. In that same manner, an application will require qualification testing, perhaps even human factors testing if it has complex key entry components. The test and evaluation should not be completed by the developer, they are too close to the product – they know where all the warts are or may not recognize them. The test and evaluation does not have to be done by a programmer, just a knowledgeable individual within the company or, again, a contracted source. Just like the original developer, any test cases and results should be part of the test and evaluation process. This will enable new changes to be regression tested as part of the acceptance of the modified application.

There are typically three people intimately involved with the development of a new product; the product champion, the product manager, and the product engineer. The product champion is most often the representative from Marketing, a person who is aware of current applications, customer base, competitor's products, and the manner in which the new product fits into the company's needs. The product champion most often is more oriented to sales than technical development (other than possibly providing market requirements early in the development process). As most marketing organizations report into the parent company, other than customer interface, they will not likely be concerned with collaborative development efforts.

The product manager will typically be from Engineering or Manufacturing. The product manager is concerned with the movement of the product through the various development stages from design, to build, to test, to integration, quality checks, and finally, shipment. There may be other activities such as beta tests, field tests, human factors testing, and so forth, depending on the complexity of the product and the variety of applications that may be found for the product. Much like the product champion, the product manager does not have to be intimately involved in the technical detail, other than how that detail can be validated, manufactured, and shipped successfully. In particular, the product manager must ensure that the organization does not impede the process through the life cycle through inaction or unnecessary delays. The product manager depends heavily on the project engineer to keep the product moving through the development cycle, and to understand the division of responsibility implied in the process.

A successful product introduction will depend heavily on the product engineer. In any project, or product introduction, one person is necessary to ensure that all the various pieces fit, are on schedule, and are within cost. That is the role of the product engineer. He, or she, will provide technical interface to vendors, quality, manufacturing engineering, field support, and marketing. The product engineer will work with vendors to establish schedules, costs, and technical understanding. From a quality perspective, the product engineer must ensure that the various parts meet quality standards and pass first article inspections. The product engineer will write, or help write, the necessary process procedures to be used in the manufacturing process. This latter task may also be in conjunction with manufacturing engineering to establish work times and work sequences. Support to field service, or field engineering, can take the form of direct technical support, field engineer training, or written procedures to assist the field engineers in their maintenance efforts. Marketing support will typically take the form of training, product brochure preparation and review, and other marketing material needed for the successful product introduction, and may even have company schools for customer training. The product engineer will establish design review dates and work with test planning through the schedule in order to maintain the proposed schedule and to ensure that the product is continuing to move in the desired direction. The bottom line is that considerable communication takes place between the product engineer and all the other interested parties, and places some burden on academia to ensure good communication skills are developed by the student.

The day of internal development and manufacturing is becoming rare these days. More and more work is being contracted, allowing the development of specialists for those skills too expensive to maintain in-house. Because of such changes, the approach to product development is being forced to become more formal and structured. The requirements for specifications, design reviews, formal schedules, documented costs, quality, and similar controls must be put into place before the actual product development is to begin. Failure to put the proper plans in place is simply a design for failure.

To be successful, collaboration takes considerable effort and planning. It requires technical knowledge, discipline, and attention to detail. Anything less is an open invitation to failure.

Other Readings

AS 9100 Manufacturing Policy Procedure, www.policyandprocedure. com, retrieved 12/21/09.

Alred, G. J., Brusaw, C. T., and Dliu, W. E. (1999). The Business Writer's Companion, 2nd Edition, Bedford/St Martins, Boston.

Beyerlein, M., S. Freedman, C. Mcgee, L. Morgan (2002). *Beyond Teams: building the collaborative organization*, Lavoisier.

Brodsky, M., (1989). *International developments in apprenticeships*, Monthly Labor Review (pgs. 40-41), U. S. Bureau of Labor Statistics, Washington, D.C.

Creating excellent manufacturing work instructions, (November 1, 1997). Modern Machine Shop, Gardner Publications, Inc.

Cross, A. (2000). Talking Business – Strategies for Successful Presentations, Prentice-Hall, Canada.

Dunford, T. (1998). *Taking the myth out of documenting work instructions*, Quality Progress.

Floyd, R. (2003). *Document Control and Release – A Two Edged Sword*. IPCC 2003 Proceedings.

Floyd, R. E. (2006). *"...but Johnny Can't Write!"*, IEEE Professional Communication Society Newsletter, September 2006.

Floyd, R. E. (2007). *"Communication 101 – Keep Your Presentations Simple"*, USA Today's Engineer, July 2007.

Greek, J., G. McCalla, J. Collins, V. Kumar, P. Meagher, J. Vassila (1998). *Supporting Peer Help and Collaboration in Distributed Workplace Environments*, International Journal of Artificial Intelligence in Education, Volume 9, pgs 159-177.

Harty, K. J. (2005). *Strategies for Business and Technical Writing*, Pearson Education, Inc.

Hennig, J. and Marita Tjarks-Sobhani (2005). *Technical Communication – international – Today and in the Future*, Verlag Schmidt-Römhild.

Hoyle, D., (2009). *Systems and Processes: Is there a difference?* Chartered Quality Institute, London, UK.

Hoyle, D., and John Thompson. *Process versus procedures*. Quality World, Chartered Quality Institute, London, UK.

Ingle, P. (2006). Think Before You Write, Pantheon Prose.

Marsen, S. (2007). Professional Writing: The Complete Guide for

Business, Industry, and IT – 2nd Edition. Palgrave-McMillan, New York.

Pfeiffer, W. S. (2001). *Technical Writing – A Practical Approach*, Prentice Hall.

Plung, D. and Tracy Montgomery (2003). *Professional Communication: The Corporate Insider's Approach,* South-Western.

Reep, D. C. (2006). *Technical Writing: Principles, Strategies, and Readings*, Pearson Education, Inc.

Riordan, D. G. (2005). Technical Report Writing Today – 9th Edition. Houghton Mifflin, Boston.

Spencer, R. (1983). *Planning, Implementation and Control in Product Test and Assurance.* Prentice-Hall, Upper Saddle River, NJ.

Spencer, R. (1983). *Computer Usability Testing and Evaluation.* Prentice-Hall, Upper Saddle River, NJ.

Spencer, R., and R. Floyd (1994). *Collaborative Writing in Product Development Across Remote Sites*, Professional Communication Conference IPCC '94, pgs. 346-350.

Spencer, R., and R. Floyd (1995). *Educating Technical Professionals to Communicate*, Professional Communication Conference IPCC '95, pgs. 152-155.

Thompson, I. (2001). *Collaboration in technical communication: a qualitative content analysis of journal articles*, 1990-1999, IEEE Transactions on Professional Communication, Volume 44, Issue 3, pgs 161-173.

Tracy, B. (2008). Speak To Win. AMACON, New York.

Wheatley, M. (July, 2006). *Work instructions: How to tell what to do,* Manufacturing Business Technology.

Chapter 8 – Intellectual Property

At its beginning, intellectual property is intangible, it cannot be seen or touched. It is the product of the mind – a concept, an idea. While it may be transformed into something tangible, it needs to be protected before that transformation, thus intellectual property law comes into being. One of the first patents issued by the United States was to Eli Whitney for the Whitney Cotton Gin. That patent was issued in 1794. In the 210 years hence, the Patent Office has issued more than 7,000,000 patents on a variety of subjects. Given that number, it would seem there might not be many things left to invent. Looking at Table 1, it is interesting to note the number of new patents for each item issued since 1976. While one patent for a pet rock doesn't seem too far-fetched, more than 500 on the common bicycle fork (the front part of the bicycle which holds the front wheel in place) is simply astounding!

Table 1 – Common Items Issued Patents Since 1976

Item Patented	Patents Issued Since 1976
Pet Rock	1
Balloons	3
Sledge Hammer	22
Hula Hoops	23
Shoe Laces	104
Hunting Arrow	122
Bicycle Fork	520

To illustrate the importance corporations place on intellectual property, International Business Machines (IBM) was issued 4,883 patents in 2009, the thirteenth consecutive year that they had received more US patents than any other company in the world. IBM's patent portfolio has more than 58,000 active patents, and this represents only a fraction of the disclosures they publish each year for additional protection (more about the value of disclosures later.)

Sometimes the concept being considered appears to be so simple it just doesn't seem worthy of being called "intellectual property". It doesn't seem worthy of the investment of applying for a utility patent to provide protection for the corporation's use of the idea. Then again, one might ask about the worthiness of the "pet rock". How many millions were sold?

What then are the various forms of intellectual property protection that a corporation may pursue? They include:

- Patents
- Trademarks
- Service Marks
- Trade Secrets
- Copyrights
- Mask Works for Semiconductors

It should be noted, most companies will have the new employee or sub-contractor sign an agreement giving the company exclusive rights to any intellectual property developed as part of work assignments. This agreement extends beyond a change in jobs, and, if not carefully avoided or limited, could cause conflict of interests in new employment situations.

Patents

Patents are issued by the United States Patent and Trademark Office (USPTO) to an individual or Corporate entity, and, after issue, provides the receiver a period of twenty years from the date of the patent application exclusive use of the patented idea. The twenty year coverage is a change from the previous period of seventeen years from date of issue. To illustrate the coverage of patents being issued today, there are several broad categories of patents; utility patents, plant patents, process patents, design patents, mask work patents, and so forth. Within the context of this book, the general use of the term patent refers to the more common form – the utility patent.

For the USPTO to issue a patent, it must meet three general inquiries in the affirmative; 1) is the invention useful and will it work for its intended purpose, 2) is the invention novel compared to prior art, and 3) is the invention non-obvious when compared to the prior art? Failing any one of the three questions is sufficient reason for the USPTO to not grant a patent. Looking back at the table previously reviewed, one must wonder how 104 patents were issued on the shoestring! As is frequently the case, there are other limitations on the patent process. For example, the concept submitted must not have been offered for sale within the prior twelve months. If it was, the concept is then considered as part of the Public Domain, and is not patentable. Good engineering records are a must when dealing with intellectual property, thus the new engineer needs to develop good habits of keeping notes, in ink, dated, and witnessed. If the protection of a patent is considered as being inappropriate for the cost benefits associated with it, an alternative approach is to publish the concept into the Public Domain. IBM did that for many years in their *IBM Technical Disclosure Bulletin*, which was replaced by *Research Disclosure* in 1998. By publishing those ideas that had not warranted the expense of a patent submission, IBM was still protected as the idea was no longer able to meet the three questions asked by the USPTO – the concept was published and had become part of the prior art, it was in the Public Domain.

One item of importance when discussing patents; when the patent is issued the protection offered by it applies only within the United States. No one can use the technology without the owner's permission within the United States, nor may they manufacture it outside of the United States and import it into the country. To do so would be considered an infringement on the patent and open to possible litigation. To obtain additional patent coverage, the owner of the patent may apply to foreign patent offices, but, in most cases, each country of interest must be individually contacted. Such protection can become very expensive. Thus, the value versus cost trade-off consideration becomes important. Some companies may "work around" a patent by manufacturing an item in another country and then distributing it world-wide, but not in the United States. While it's a legal approach, one might question the ethics of such practices.

Several years the USPTO determined that computer software could not be patented (the determination was that a patent would unduly restrict the use of program languages and operating systems). Given that, the USPTO did acknowledge the uniqueness of applications developed for specific purposes or processes. Such software applications can be granted patent protection.

There is one other avenue open to provide limited patent protection called a provisional patent. The provisional patent is a device instituted by the USPTO that allows a less formal application on a possibly patentable subject to be submitted, registered, and date stamped. The effect of this submission is that it provides a twelve-month window for a formal utility application to be submitted, where the utility submission will take advantage of the earlier provisional patent filing date. In this case, the provisional patent provides a twelve month window during which the person, or corporation, can investigate, experiment, or otherwise develop a concept before deciding on whether or not it is financially justifiable for the cost of the utility application. The cost of the provisional patent is a fraction of the issue cost of a patent. The caveat to the provisional patent is that it provides only a twelve-month protection period, and cannot be extended. If the person, or company, wished to extend protection, a "new" provisional would have to be submitted – as an independent provisional patent, again reflecting a new twelve month period of protection. If an utility patent were then submitted, it could only claim the time period of the second provisional patent, not the original date of the first submitted. It should also be noted, that the USPTO makes no investigation in the patentability of the item covered in the provisional patent, it merely assigns a number and date stamps the submission.

Trademarks

The general purpose of a trademark is to provide instant recognition of a company or product. Trademarks are formal forms of recognition and are registered by the USPTO. Similar protection is provided with a trademark as a patent, and the owner of the trademark can pursue infringement suits against other organizations using similar marks or improperly using the registered mark. For example, the trademark IBM should be formally marked with the registered trademark symbol (®), at least once within a document, with the footnote; "IBM is a registered trademark of International Business Machines, White Plains, NY". In other words, it would appear as IBM˚, with the appropriate footnote. A company, or individual, can also place an informal mark on the logo, acronym, or other selected identifier, the ™, indicating that trademark rights are claimed, thus providing a warning to others that any use should be restricted or avoided. Trademarks have, at times, become so common that the trademark itself becomes the reference. Consider, "Please make me a Xerox copy." Here the name of the company and its process has been used because of their leadership early on in the photocopy industry. If one were to make a photocopy on a Sony or Toshiba copier, than it couldn't be a Xerox copy, could it? Most companies are very sensitive to such common use, and will pursue litigation to stop such abuses of their trademark. Fortunately, or unfortunately, such is sometimes the price of that "instant recognition" being sought.

There is a second mark, the service mark, which is essentially the same as the trademark, except by the USPTO definition is used to represent a service offering rather than a product offering. For example, "Your T-Bar Roofing Specialist." could be used as a service mark for a company with business interests in the repair of home or business roofs. The paperwork is essentially the same as is the process by the USPTO. Once the mark is issued, it may be identified by the service mark symbol, SM, or the registered symbol, ®.

Trademarks and service marks, once issued, have a practically unlimited lifetime. The owner must re-new, or confirm continuous use, at the end of five years and ten years after issue, and every ten years thereafter. Each time the renewal fee is submitted, the owner must also provide evidence of the on-going use.

Copyrights

Where patents provide protection of products, copyrights provide a level of protection where the item being protected is a work of art or other creative endeavor (book, film, video, sculpture, computer program, etc.) Where a patent has to be applied for, researched, and then issued by the USPTO, an intangible copyright exists at the moment of creation of the subject work. That intangible copyright may be formalized through the submission of a copyright application to the Register of Copyrights. The cost and process are much less involved versus the patent, and can easily be accomplished by an individual without resorting to an attorney.

A copyright remains in force for the life of the author plus seventy years. As the holder of a copyright, you can:

- Replicate the content of the copyrighted material
- Create new materials based upon the original
- Distribute or sell copies of the material
- Display or perform the material publicly

Because of Fair Use laws, others can use portions of copyrighted material for non-commercial purposes. In broad terms, copyrighted material cannot be photocopied, scanned, or otherwise copied.

Computer programs offer some unique challenges. One argument is that computer software is a language, and as such, cannot be patent or copyright protected. Other arguments have been put forth that algorithms or similar code fits the copyright requirements, and novel processes may fit patent requirements. The book remains open in the area of computer programming protection, and, with the on-going development of web-based code and structures, will probably become more complex in the years to follow. In most instances today, companies will, at a minimum, copyright their programs. As noted earlier, the USPTO does allow software processes to apply for patent protection.

Trade Secrets

One of the first criteria for a trade secret is that it must be secret! If it is a secret, then how does one garner protection for it? While it seems somewhat *Catch 22*, trade secrets do exist. Perhaps the best-kept trade secret is the formula for *Coke' Classic*. As long as the secret is maintained, controlled, and otherwise kept from the public domain, it is a secret. Once the secret becomes public knowledge, there is no protection provided on the subject. At that point, the owner may wish to seek patent or copyright protection as appropriate. The USPTO has given patent protection in some cases where the original owner could demonstrate that a particular concept had been treated as a Trade Secret for some period of time prior to the disclosure – again depending on formal records showing the protection that had been given that concept. There is no federal government agency tasked with trade secret registration or enforcement.

Other Protections

There are a number of other patent types that most people, unless working in highly specialized careers, will not come into contact with. For example, within the agriculture industry patents are granted for new varieties of existing plant families, new spores, and other distinctive growths new to the industry. There is patent protection for artistic designs to be placed on other articles being manufactured. The design patents are also distinct in that their legal life is only fourteen years as opposed to the twenty years afforded other patents. There is on-going development in the area of biotechnology with DNA modifications. Is the resultant plant or animal a new breed (not normal within the context of what exists today), and thus enabled to apply for protection under patent law? There have also been extensions of copyright law, where the masks associated with computer chip manufacture can be copyright protected under certain conditions. The law concerning chip masks, Chip Act of 1984, provides protection to the owner with some facets of copyright and some of patents. Mask protection has a protection period of ten years.

Intellectual property is extremely important to businesses today. It can be a considerable investment (consider the cost to IBM to have issued over 3,000 patents each year), but the return may be several orders of magnitude over the cost. The patent can provide direct contribution to the corporate revenue stream through license fees, and the patent may also provide a competitive advantage of one company over its competitors – they cannot take advantage of the newly patented technology.

It is important that all engineers understand the importance of intellectual property, both to the engineer's and the corporation's benefit. Most corporations provide some type of recognition for patents issued, and it is always a good addition to one's resume. Take time to understand the corporate needs, the technology in which it works, and submit that little idea ...it may become famous as the pet rock of tomorrow!

In years past, while teaching in the graduate program at a southern university, there seemed to be a standard approach to the start of each semester. The students would immediately ask, "What are the important equations for this class?" The question might also be along the lines, "What are the important topics we should study?" Of course, the stock answer could have been, "Everything we teach you is important", but that might have been a bit pretentious on our part. We would begin our explanation to the class by stating that there would not be any tests. The grade for the semester would be derived from their effort on a term paper (which almost always prompted a reduction in class size the second night). After that, we would write a simple equation on the board, noting to the students that it would be the most important thing they could take from the class:

$$I + I + I = S \qquad (1)$$

You could almost hear the wheels begin to churn, $3I = S$?

As we began our lecture, we told the young engineering students that most of them would be employed in industry, and that, for the most part, they would be expected to solve problems. The problems could range from the mundane and simple, to something exotic, something out of this world, something not yet invented! What would be expected of them was to provide *solutions* to problems, thus in the equation, S equals *Solutions*. The success of each one of the students would depend on how well they solved the problems given them. The solution, like the problems, could range from the simple to the complex. The most important thing was to remember to look at the problem from different perspectives to make sure the solution offered represented the best technical answer for the most cost effective investment. Another casual reminder was that the most elegant solution may not be the best, always try for simplicity if possible. Simple solutions can frequently provide success in terms of cost, time, and effect.

Having given the introduction and the goal of the class (to formulate solutions), we would then set the parameters for the student's class project – any product assembly using robot assembly techniques. They were to describe the product and the general conditions of parts presentation, limiting factors, and any other problems expected in the implementation of their project in the real world. While they could work alone, we suggested two or three people teams (another way to get them used to working with teams when they moved into industry). At that point, we introduced them to the automation project to be discussed as part of the class, and the first "I" – Imagination.

To begin any project, the engineer must look at the requirements and specifications, and let their imagination begin to explore possible solutions. The solution can be built on past experience, as long as that experience is built on "ten years experience", not "one year of experience ten times". The engineer needs to break out of the mold of "That's the way we have always done it", that syndrome that says "It's too risky, you'll never succeed." Stretch the imagination, break out of the paradigm that keeps so many frozen into the narrow path of mediocrity. Of course, this is not meant to imply that only new thoughts and new approaches are to be used, there are many tools and approaches that have stood the test of years. For example, shaker bowls (a vibrating parts orientation and feeding device) have been used for years as part orientation and presentation devices in automated manufacturing lines. However, might it be cheaper and just as effective to have the supplier of the part provide the part in sticks or tape fed rolls, already oriented and ready for quick presentation? Another aspect of using the imagination is that one doesn't have to focus on the tooling to be used in the final solution. Why not look at the product, or proposed product, to see if part changes could be made to facilitate automated assembly? Where there are screws, could pop fit or press fit anchors serve as well? This provides not only an easier method for assembly, but also cuts down on parts cost, feeders, and presentation methods. It is the imagination that has driven mankind to many wonderful successes – use it to help in the development of product solutions.

One final thought on imagination as it applies to engineering. Imagination cannot be taught, but engineers can be taught to "think outside the box", they can be taught to examine the problem being worked outside the paradigm of the problem itself. That reminds us of the story about an engineering problem that happened a number of years ago. A new power plant was being built, and the contractor had finished the area scheduled to house the very large generators, not yet installed. When it came time to move the generators into place, much to the contractor's chagrin, the cranes used to place the generators couldn't fit through the opening to place the generator bases over the pre-set bolts in the concrete floor. A number of approaches were suggested, ranging from cutting off the bolts and sliding the units in (and, of course, then drilling and anchoring the units in place), to removing the roof and dropping the units into place, or to using rollers to roll the units into place (but the bolts on the floor halted that discussion). The final solution, suggested by an engineer using his (it may have been a "her") imagination – flood the floor with water covering the height of the bolts and freeze it! The generators were slid into place, and as the water thawed, gently lowered onto the bolts. Simple - but outside the box.

Having developed the general concept or approach to the project, the students were ready to begin the design of the workstation, and it was time to introduce them to the second "I" in the equation – Innovation. In the process of designing an automation center, or tool, the engineer may find that the proposed solution is too expensive, too large, too...(pick another superlative), and an alternative must be found. The engineer must look at the product and the proposed solution and come up with alternatives, new innovative ways to address the problem at hand. One project we worked on had four bolts coming through the bottom of the mounting plate into tapped holes to fasten the unit onto the base. The proposed solutions had vibratory feeders, nut drivers, and fixtures for presentation (right side up, sideways, and even up-side down.) None of the proposed solutions were particularly elegant or cost effective.

In this particular project, it was decided to look at the case itself to see if a press fit/snap fit solution might be applicable. Where the four bolts came through, the mold was redesigned to have four plastic "bolts" molded in place, with a slot in each bolt near the case bottom to use as a retainer. The part being mounted into the base had the tapped holes removed and a simple opening stamped out which fit down over the plastic bolts on the base. As the part was pressed into place, the plastic bolts moved through the four holes, and, when it bottomed out, "snap", the unit was held firmly in place – a simple yet elegant solution. Innovation provides a different perspective, another way at looking at what needs to be done without letting all manner of restrictions prevent the engineer from reaching a satisfactory solution.

Sometimes our students would note that imagination and innovation seemed to be similar in approach to product solutions. We would tell them they were correct in their view, but that we looked at the two with a fine line of difference as we employed the words. From our perspective, imagination can provide solutions and approaches using technology not yet in existence, some discovery must yet happen. If one looks at the authors of fifty years ago, how much of the science fiction is now reality? Their's was a world of pure imagination, found daily in our world of reality today. Innovation, on the other hand, concerns the adaptation of existing materials to the problem solution, albeit in a manner not previously considered.

In many projects, imagination and innovation are enough to provide the needed solution. There are others, where the solution just can't be arrived at with existing technology, parts, and devices. Another approach is needed, thus the final "I" – Invention. Invention is something new, untried, not yet fully developed, more a concept than something concrete, yet offering an approach to the solution needed. Can it be done? Can technology support the concept? All these questions need to be answered in the process of moving the inventive concept from the drawing board to the manufacturing floor (and one must not forget the process of protecting intellectual property rights and filing the invention application with the United States Patent and Trademark Office or the equivalent patenting office in other countries). Invention is the most difficult of the "I's" to implement. It cannot be scheduled or looked up in a textbook. The answer may be hidden or simply not obtainable, given the state of technology at the time. Invention frequently calls upon the first two "I's", requiring both imagination and innovation to arrive at some new concept, approach, or method. It must also be recognized that invention carries with it the greatest risk of failure – it hasn't yet been tried and proven to be a success. As a result, the process of generating a solution may be slowed considerably if the solution depends on successfully inventing a critical part or process. It has been said that invention is difficult to schedule, so don't depend on it!

A number of years ago we had the opportunity to work on a project that was attempting to automate the handling of silicon wafers in a clean room, in this case a Class 10 clean room (no more than 10 one micron particles per cubic meter of air). It was decided that a new robot would be designed for operation in the clean room environment, which, in itself, was a challenge. All of the moving mechanical joints, drives, and other moving parts had to be encased in shrouds to prevent any metal or dust escaping into the clean space around the wafers. The handling of the wafer itself presented the greatest challenge, as mechanical claws could not be used over the surface or used to grasp the edges of the wafer for fear of chipping or dislodging particles in the process. The final solution, an invention, was a metal claw that moved air (clean air) across the surface of the wafer, lifting the wafer in a Bernoulli effect with nothing coming into contact with the wafer.

We always found it interesting to watch the students wrestle with the three concepts of Imagination, Innovation, and Invention as they worked through the solution to their particular project. We did permit "inventions" to be included, even when we didn't have time to prove or disprove the viability of any particular one. Obviously, in industry, that would have to be carried out in the process of moving to the final solution. It was also interesting to watch the teams develop, each calling on particular skills offered by individual team members – a valuable lesson in itself.

About mid-way through the semester, we offered one minor modification to the base equation stated earlier. We called it the OBTW factor, so the equation now looked like:

$$OBTW \ (I + I + I) = S \qquad (2)$$

Most students just scratched their heads. OBTW? We explained to them the acronym stood for words that they would hear many times, in one form or another, during their career. As projects began to reach their conclusions, or even during production, someone from Purchasing could call and say, "Oh, by the way the vendor supplying part A just went out of business, and the replacement vendor part isn't the same size or mounted in the same manner." Suddenly a panic on how the process, fixtures, and other parts of the system will require changes to fit the new part. Part of that panic may be on deciding how and when to implement the change, as the process has parts in inventory for the present build method. "Oh, by the way...", words that seem so innocent, yet can destroy many months of work on a new process or product. The words can come from Marketing, Purchasing, Legal, Development, Manufacturing, or Field Service. Sometimes the particular object of the words can be evaluated and not done, however, most times the fateful uttering will cause some panic at the worst possible moment in the development process. In the process of developing a robot application in the class, we used the phrase each Monday to introduce a modification that was going to be required for the product being built (in this case a power supply). In one case it might be the need to rotate a particular part 180 degrees, or move it to a different location. In another case, where a part had originally had a straight line approach to insertion, a new obstruction would be added, causing the path of the placement robot to be modified. By the time the semester ended, the students would start the Monday class by asking, "Oh, by the way, what change do we have to deal with tonight?" Many years later, we would run across a prior student, who would almost always greet us with "Oh, by the way Professor..." We believe the lesson stuck!

The answers are not always in the textbooks, nor are there always equations that fit the particular problem at hand. It would be nice if it were so, but more frequently than not, human ingenuity is called upon in the final analysis. Imagination, Innovation, and Invention are all concepts an engineer will have to continue to apply to problems faced over the years. There aren't any equations involved in any of the three. There aren't any boundaries in place to limit where the engineer's mind may go in applying the three concepts and solving the particular need of the moment. This is not meant as a disparity on textbooks or the equations taught in school – they are needed as the foundation for our learning. Given the need for such, the concepts discussed in this chapter are more appropriate in understanding approaches in the application of the knowledge gained, and to place emphasis on the need for thinking not simply re-iterating facts. This may prove to be a challenge for some who wish everything was tightly bound, with equations to apply for any given circumstance. Unfortunately, people with this approach are due for many painful experiences over their life, and may wish to consider other fields of endeavor. The successful engineer will understand the concepts and the equations, and will know when to apply them, even when faced with "Oh, by the way..."

Other Readings

DeMatteis, R. (2005). *From Patent to Profit*. Square One Publishers, Garden City Park, NY.

Floyd, R. E. (2005). *"Such a simple idea..."*. IEEE Potentials, April/May 2005.

Floyd, R. E. (2006). *"The Three I's in Solutions"*. IEEE Potentials, September/October 2006.

Floyd, R. E. (2006). "Such a simple idea...", International Engineering Management Conference, September 2006.

Herrington, T. K. (2003). *A Legal Primer for the Digital Age*. Pearson Longman, New York.

Rockman, H. B. (2004). *Intellectual Property Law for Engineers and Scientists*. Wiley, Hoboken, NJ.

Chapter 9 – Ethics and Mentors

Ethics

The question is, what ethics, if any, are expected of engineers? Perhaps the few noted by the Boy Scouts of America as an individual being honest, trustworthy, loyal, etc. are simple enough for consideration. What other things could be expected of an engineer, other than a sound technical education and good judgment? Besides, aren't ethics more appropriate to the medical professions and legal professions? Then again, considering some of the problems found in legal systems, perhaps ethics no longer apply there.

Frequently there is some confusion between the word ethics and the word morals. In simplistic terms, morals refer more to the individual's system of conduct to determine whether something is right or wrong, good or bad. Individual morals are usually fixed early in life, changing little over the years. Ethics more refers to a field of philosophy describing a social system in which morals are applied, where there may be written standards or codes that belong to a group. As an example, the IEEE has written a Code of Ethics for its membership, where the code expounds on the expectations of the Society and the responsibilities placed on the membership as being good community citizens. Another example is offered by the Society of Manufacturing Engineers (SME) where in their Code of Ethics is given the Canons of Professional Conduct – another list of expectations of the membership on behalf of the Society. The National Society of Professional Engineers (NSPE) also offers a Code of Ethics, one that has been implemented by states as a Code of Ethics for licensed engineers. In this case, the violation of the Code can result in revocation of the engineer's professional license. Finally, the IEEE offers a Students Ethics Competition, sponsored by the IEEE Ethics and Member Conduct Committee. It has been developed for use at IEEE

Regional events to encourage the study and awareness of professional ethics. The competition has three objectives: 1) to foster familiarity with the IEEE Code of Ethics, 2) to promote a model for discussion of ethical questions, and 3) to provide experience in applying ethical concepts to professional situations. In general, one's morals do not change over time, but the Code of Ethics may dictate different interpretations from a societal perspective over time as attitudes and acceptances change.

It is interesting for the student or practicing engineer to read their Society's Code of Ethics. One of the first things that will be noted is that the statements in the Code are not generally expressed in specific terms, more as goals to be achieved. For example, the second in the list of ten items in the IEEE Code of Ethics reads, "to avoid real or perceived conflicts of interest whenever possible, and to disclose them to affected parties when they do exist." In this case, it could have been stated "to avoid conflicts of interest", but that then sidesteps the key word "perceived", as the perception of conflict may vary from person to person, depending on their interests or special needs. Other key words in this statement are "whenever possible", as there may be instances where a conflict of interest could exist, but knowledge of the conflict is highly classified or restricted to the point that the conflict cannot be divulged. Does this then violate the code of ethics, or is it an extension of the "whenever possible" caveat?

While all ten elements of the IEEE's Code of Ethics are important and may impact many facets of daily life and career steps, the seventh is one that frequently gets ignored or, at the worst, violated, that it is worth noting. In the seventh, it states, "to seek, accept, and offer honest criticism of technical work, to acknowledge and correct errors, and to *credit properly the contributions of others.*" If a student buys a term paper from a library of term papers rather than writing it, or allows someone else to write a paper for them, this is dishonest and violates the spirit of the ethical conduct item. Similarly, copying or extracting work of others without proper recognition constitutes plagiarism, again violating the spirit of the ethical conduct item. In addition, such plagiarism may violate federal intellectual property copyright protection afforded the original author, placing the student in jeopardy of prosecution.

Most rules given in any Society's Code of Ethics are primarily common sense applications for moral actions by the individual. Honesty, responsibility, accountability, fair treatment, avoidance of injury to others, etc., all describe ethical obligations that the engineer accepts in the role they have chosen as a career. It is much the same for military academies where honor, duty, and country take the center stage for their credos of ethics. Take time to look into the Societies belonged to and understand their particular Code of Ethics, and how it can help direct day to day activity as a career is pursued. If, someday, someone asks if there is a Code of Ethics for Engineers, you will be able to not only answer in the affirmative, but also help them understand the expectations being placed on them through such codes.

Mentors

As you stand on that graduation platform with your degree in your hand, you believe you are now educated, knowledgeable, experienced, and ready to conquer the world. Well, perhaps not quite the world, but ready to take on the responsibilities of an engineer, gaining fame and riches along the way. You are on your way to climb to the top of that pillar of success and financial reward – your career! A word of caution before you begin some Don Quixote charge, there may be a few bumps along the way you need to anticipate.

One of the first things you will learn as you begin your new career is that your experience base is typically sadly lacking fundamental knowledge for successful completion of some assignments. You may find the theory you were taught in school doesn't quite map to the problem you have been given, it *almost* fits but not quite. You find you have to accommodate some of the rules you learned with a small dose of practicality to obtain the ultimate solution. This is known as *experience.* Tuck it away for future reference, you will probably be able to use the approach, solution, or some modification of it in other applications you will be assigned in the future. The lack of experience will come into play for a number of projects and assignments until you find you have spent 3 to 10 years in the quest of your career. Suddenly, you find yourself one of those *experienced* engineers that others are looking for. The length of time will vary based on the type of engineer, the projects assigned, and the ability of the engineer to absorb the requisite knowledge. Could there be a better way than to slowly slog your way project by project, adding to your experience base bit by bit? One approach may be through association with a *mentor* (or mentors).

In the classical sense, a mentor is assigned to assist more junior members of the organization learn what is necessary to move quickly to become a productive member of the group. The mentor may provide technical assistance or procedural assistance as the situation dictates. In most assignments, the mentor is not assigned to complete the work, but to make sure the new engineer is making safe and reasonable progress toward a solution (and to provide suggestions when a certain approach is headed for a disaster!). One experience gained along the way is stopping to consider, in depth, when the mentor says, "Have you considered…"? There may be a subtle gem of wisdom hidden in that question. At some point, the junior member may become a mentor in their own right. Mentors may be assigned when new engineers come into an organization, and, then again, they may not, leaving it to the new engineer to development such relations on their own. Just how might one go about that?

As a new member of an organization, the first things to do is look at the other engineers in the group and try to understand their particular assignments. The older engineers are more likely to be good candidates for the mentor role, but care must be taken – some old engineers are simply waiting on retirement! They probably won't be terribly interested, or effective, in taking on the mentor role, so drop them from consideration. The term "older" may also be misleading, as that "older" engineer to act as a mentor may be a relative new engineer who has had benefit of a strong mentor relationship, has completed a string of successful projects, and is obviously enthusiastic about the job. In the search for a possible mentor, look for the person other engineers are constantly going to for answers. There is probably a sound basis for that, say *experience and a willingness to share*?

The experience and willingness to share says quite a bit about the strength of an individual. They have garnered the experience, over a number of years and projects, and have the positive self-worth which allows them to share that experience with others who ask. The willingness to share is a critical attribute for a good mentor selection. As the new engineer finds that person who is willing to accept an interruption on their own project, taking time to provide direction, or, more importantly, provide discussion and act as a sounding board on a particular problem, they have probably discovered a good mentor candidate. With such an approach, the mentor is pushing the new engineer into ways of accomplishing the needed task without the mentor *doing* it. The new engineer, in the process of looking, may also find that the mentor of interest can no longer work with differential equations, may not remember all of the magnetic flux equations, or any number of theoretical topics the new engineer just finished in school last semester. How can that be? What the new engineer is about to discover is that there is a vast body of information covered in school that may not find application in industry. There are many reasons, the foremost being that the majority of projects will not require formal, theoretical research and development, merely a solution that works. As a result, what is remembered most often are the things that work, not the theory behind it. That does not mean to imply the mentor cannot refresh that knowledge given some period of time to dig back through the text books. It just hasn't been important enough to maintain its currency in memory.

Another thing the new engineer may note, there are times when multiple mentors may come into play, or a new mentor is needed. Most often this happens as new projects, with new problems, are undertaken, and the help needed has a different emphasis or knowledge base need. As a result, the new engineer may find, over the years, a number of people (mentors) will provide guidance and assistance in successful career development. In most cases, each new mentor is easier to find – the knowledge base of the new engineer is gaining insight into what makes a good mentor!

Soon after being transferred to the testing laboratory from his original field assignment, Spencer found himself being mentored as a result of the dedicated attitude he brought to his new assignment in Product Test. His following assignments were challenging and interesting. After some years, the same manager offered Spencer the opportunity to be part of the planning tem for a new laboratory in another state. In the process, Spencer was able to convince the architect to make essential changes in design of the new testing laboratory. At a later point, he was instrumental in receiving a promotion and an opportunity to rewrite the Division's Management Manual. You never know what may come of a mentoring experience. In Spencer's case, he benefitted from his mentor, and, in turn, had over the years reached out to mentor others as he progressed in product test and management.

The outcome of the process is intended to assist the new engineer into becoming a valued and productive member of the industrial team. Such success reflects good practices on the organization in training new members, and on the new engineer in accepting guidance along the way to learn how to contribute to the team's success. One other outcome that may not be immediately recognized – the new engineer may turn into one of those grizzled veteran engineers and become a mentor for the next budding young engineer.

Grab yourself a mentor – and, perhaps, consider becoming one for future graduates.

Other Readings

DesJardins, J. (2010). *"An Introduction to Business Ethics, Fourth Edition"*. McGraw Hill, Columbus, OH.

Floyd, R. E. (2010). *"Find Yourself A Mentor!"*, IEEE Potentials, July/ August 2010.

Gert, B. (1988). *Morality: A New Justification of the Moral Rules*. Oxford University Press, New York.

Howard, R. A. and C. D. Koruv (2008). *Ethics for the Real World: Creating a Personal Code to Guide Decisions in Work and Life*. Harvard Business Press, Boston.

Jamieson, Dale (2008). *Ethics and the Environment: An Introduction*. Cambridge University Press, Cambridge, UK.

Maxwell, John C. (2005). *Ethics 101: What Every Leader Needs to Know*. ISBN 0-446-57809-6.

Missner, M. (1980). *Ethics of the Business System*. Alfred Publishing Co., Van Nuys, CA.

Pfeiffer, Raymond S. and Ralph P. Forsberg (2005). *Ethics on the Job: Cases and Strategies, 3rd Edition*. Wadsworth, Belmont, CA.

Singer, P. (1979). *Practical Ethics*. Cambridge University Press, Cambridge, UK.

Singer, P. (2000). *Writings on an ethical life*. Harper Collins Publishers, London, UK.

Williams, Bernard (1972). *Morality: An Introduction to Ethics*. Cambridge University Press, Cambridge, UK.

Zaphiropoulos, R. (2010). *Entrepreneurial Wisdom – Philosophical Thoughts for an Uncluttered Life*. iUniverse, Inc., New York.

Appendix A – Sample Report Format

Reports have a number of functions ranging from technical reports, investigative reports, special studies, and the like. In most cases, a report will have common features included, however, there may exist a corporate style requirement and existing reports, so questions should be asked during the preparation phase. The following is a general sample report format, found commonly in industry.

Title Page

The Title Page should have a common name or key point that identifies the general report content. For example, it could be "Special Investigation Into The Effects of Low Viscosity Oil At High Temperatures". Included on the title page should be the name of the author(s), the date of the report release, and some identifier (TR-11001, ER-00099, etc.) to more easily reference or retrieve the report from archives. If there is confidential material included within the report, a footnote identifying that fact should be included along with the name or position of the individual who can authorize release of the material. The report may also be marked as Company Confidential or Management Confidential as appropriate.

Executive Summary

The intent of the Executive Summary is to provide the reader with a one page summary, most often no more than four paragraphs. The paragraphs will provide a short background of the reason for the report, the analysis of the investigation, any conclusions drawn from the review, and, finally, any recommendations based on the review. Charts, pictures, etc. are not usually found within the summary. It should be limited to one page, and since it is based on the supporting document it should be the last part of the report to be written (much of the Executive Summary can be a cut-and-paste from the body of the report).

Background

The Background is a summary of the problem, event, or cause for the activity associated with the report. It should be in depth sufficiently for the reader to understand the events, or other reasons for the actions to be undertaken. Events, places, people, dates, etc. should all be included in this section. Summary charts may also be included, but data charts or lengthy illustrations should be included in an Appendix, thus not presenting a lot of clutter that the reader has to move through in the body of the report. By placing volumes of data in the Appendix, the reader can, if they wish, look to the greater depth.

Actions Taken

Based on the problem background, what were the plans to be undertaken to investigate the problem. The Action Taken may be a special test, a survey, a field investigation, or any number of activities that will attempt to gain an understanding of the problem of interest. Any special equipment, training, survey, construction, and similar activities planned to be undertaken should be described in detail in this section. Individuals, companies, or other sources of support during the investigation should be included in this section. Large amounts of data, pictures, survey forms, and the like should be included as an Appendix.

Conclusions

What was learned from the actions taken? Conclusions may have been reached that basically find no problem. If there are positive results from testing, field visits, surveys, or other activity undertaken, what conclusions can be drawn? Summary charts, photographs, and short tables to support the stated conclusions may be included in this section, but detailed data should be moved to an Appendix.

Recommendations

Based on the Conclusions, what actions are recommended? The recommendation may be to do nothing – the problem isn't important enough to spend resources on, or there may be a series of recommendations that have a priority or phase identified. All recommendations should be included in the Executive Summary (no new recommendations should show up there). In general, there will be no charts, pictures, etc. in this section. If there are a series of recommendations to be phased in, the time relationships may be included here.

Appendices

Multiple appendices may be appropriate, i.e. data charts, equipment used, products tested, organizations/personnel lists, pictures, and so forth. In some instances, the amount of data may preclude inclusion in the Appendices, but may be referenced as being found in Test File XXX for those who wish to view the complete data file.

Motor Failures

November 11, 2010

History

- No unusual motor failures past 3 years

- Motor failures started in January in Texas

- Motor failures started in March in Argentina

- No other locations with significant motor failures

Failure Analysis

- Teflon insulation melted, allowing short circuit

- Epoxy used to hold windings in place melted

- Bottom Hole Temperatures estimated at 350 to 400 degrees F (within motor operating temperature specification)

Failure Analysis (Continued)

- No Down Hole Sensors available due to high Bottom Hole Temperatures

- Failing motors built in 2 different plants, same process procedure and parts

- Epoxy and teflon insulation certified by vendor

Possible Causes

- Bottom Hole Temperature higher than estimated

- Epoxy cure incomplete allowing green epoxy failure

- Manufacturing/Installation differences

Review

- Bottom hole temperatures of 400F coupled with typical motor temperature rise during operation could see operating temperature near 470F, upper limit of normal operation

- Operation within expected parameters

Review (Continued)

- Epoxy curing process reviewed with vendor, and process met all vendor requirements for proper cure

- Properly cured epoxy rated at operating temperatures to over 700F

Review (Continued)

- One change in manufacturing/installation process noted at both locations, a new vendor motor oil was being used

- New vendor oil met oil specification

- New vendor oil is $15 per gallon cheaper

Test

- Several vendor oils to be subjected to high temperature test (to 500F)

- Samples of epoxy, teflon insulation, and other insulation to be subjected to high temperature oil

- Test temperature to range from 300F to 500F

Results

- 7 vendor oils tested

- 5 vendor oils passed the test with no failures noted

- 2 vendor oils failed, with decomposition of both the epoxy and teflon. One was the new vendor oil.

Results (Continued)

- 2 failing vendor oils contained esters as part of the chemical make-up

- Esters separated (de-bonded) at operating temperatures of approximately 415-425F

- Esters caused the epoxy and teflon failures

Solution

- Modified motor oil specification to exclude ester and/or di-esters

- Return all of the vendor oil to the manufacturer

- Drain and re-fill all motors in stock containing the particular vendor oil

Conclusion

- No new failures in motors in Texas and Argentina since the oil change was implemented

- Any proposed new oil will have to be certified by the vendor to maximum operating temperature (including motor rise) plus 50F

Appendix C – Sample Test Plan

As previously noted, testing of most products will be done in three phases, or points within the development process, with an Engineering model, a pre-production model, and with a first Manufacturing model. In each phase, testing will follow the same set of tests, with the possible exception of the Field Test which is most often completed with Manufacturing level equipment. In this appendix, the Test Plan sample is given at two levels, an overall Test Plan, and then one of the specific tests to be conducted expanded upon (all levels of the overall will be expanded in the final Test Plan being used).

General Test Plan

Introduction – Brief description of the product in test.

Model and Name – This could be the actual model name or the Development code name.

Revision Level – Phase dependent revision level, may vary from phase to phase.

Specification Level – Date and revision level of Product Specification referenced by tests.

Tester and Test Date(s) – Who did the testing and when.

Tests to be completed – A description and plan for specific tests to be completed.

- Functional – any specific unit tests, software, peripheral equipment, etc. tests (each will have a level specific test plan and associated test scripts where needed).
- Classical – classical testing such as THA, ESD, RFI, EMD, PLT, PLD, Acoustics, Vibration, etc. (each will have level specific test plan and associated test scripts where needed).
- Documentation – evaluation(s) to be performed on documenta-

tion, including identification of specific documents required for product release (each document will have specific test plan and associated test scripts where needed).

- Usability – identified usability testing, including skill levels, number of test personnel, environments, documentation requirements, etc. (each will have level specific test plan and associated test scripts where needed).
- Training – identified evaluation of training planned, including effectiveness as determined during the Serviceability Test (if more than one training program, each will have level specific test plan and associated test scripts where needed).
- Serviceability – identified service technician skill levels, documentation, tools, diagnostic software level, method of evaluation, etc. (specific test plans and associated test scripts where needed).
- Field Tests – as determined by evaluation of laboratory tests and test results, determine need, location(s), duration, specific requirements, etc. (specific test plans and associated evaluation methods).

The identified set of tests to be completed will be repeated for all three test phases, however the level of tests, documentation, test specifics may vary as the product moves through the development process.

Serviceability Test Plan

Introduction – A brief description of the testing to be accomplished by this Test Plan.

Model and Name – This could be the actual model name or the Development code name.

Revision Level – Phase dependent revision level, may vary from phase to phase.

Documentation – Service document(s) to be tested including revision level(s).

Training – Identification of required training prior to the test(s).

Tester and Test Date(s) – Who did the testing and when.

Tests to be completed – A description and plan for specific tests to be completed.

- Installation – Product installation using Service or User documentation (specific test scripts where needed).

- Access - With covers on, remove necessary covers to evaluate ease of access for part removal, replacement, and/or adjustment (specific test scripts where needed).
- Adjustments – Make adjustments, and assess ease and accuracy of adjustments (specific test scripts where needed).
- Replacements – Replace all Field Replaceable Units (FRU) and assess ease of parts/unit replacements (specific test scripts where needed).
- Fault Isolation – Install predetermined list of known problems to assess the completeness and accuracy of troubleshooting support documentation (specific test scripts where needed).

Did the unit function properly following the above actions? If so, then report that fact, and state position of support for unit entering the next production phase.

If the unit did not function properly, why not? (describe clearly the nature and cause of the problems). Also report on the level of ease/difficulty involved along with any recommendations for improving ease of doing servicing. Note - It is Engineering's final responsibility to determine problem solutions.

Appendix D – Sample Test Script

```
* * * * * * * * * * * * * * * * * * * * * * * * * * * * * * * * * * * * * * *
```
* Test Name – Ship Test *
* Test Equipment Used – THA Chamber, Model AC1, Serial Number 77445 *
* Equipment In Test – Model 73, Touch Sensitive Display, Serial Number 008, Rev C *
* Software Used In Test – Touch Screen Diagnostic, Rev 1.4 *
* Test Script ID – THA 27, Rev 2.3 *
* Date(s) of Test - _____ Conducted By - _____ *
* Test Purpose – The purpose of this test is to determine that the unit under test will perform *
* after being subjected to both HIGH and LOW shipping temperatures as specified in the *
* unit technical specification. The unit will be subjected to each temperature specified for a *
* period of 24 hours, allowed to return to normal operating room temperature, and then *
* subjected to the test routine as given in the software in use. *
* Equipment Technical Specification – 00-73-0003, 11-11-11, Rev H *
* Specification Temperatures – High <u>120 F</u> Low <u>-40 F</u> *
```
* * * * * * * * * * * * * * * * * * * * * * * * * * * * * * * * * * * * * * *
```

PRELIMINARY WORK –

1. Install unit in test in the THA, centering the unit on a work bench with access to all sides of the unit in test.
2. Record the room ambient temperature - <u>67.5 F</u>
3. Turn the unit in test to the ON condition, and run the test software as identified in the Software Used In Test. If there are any problems detected, stop the test and go to the FINAL section of this script. Otherwise, turn the system in test to the OFF condition and continue to the next phase.

HIGH TEMPERATURE TEST -

1. Set the control of the THA to the specified high temperature for shipping plus 10%.
2. Allow the THA to reach the temperature setting.

3. Maintain the stable temperature for a period of 24 hours.
4. At the end of the 24 hour period, allow the unit in test to again return to ambient room temperature.
5. Record the room ambient temperature - <u>68.1 F</u>
6. Turn the unit in test to the ON condition, and run the test software as identified in the Software Used In Test. If there are any problems detected, stop the test and go to the FINAL section of this script. Otherwise, turn the system in test to the OFF condition and continue to the next phase.

LOW TEMPERATURE TEST
1. Set the control of the THA to the specified high temperature for shipping minus 10%.
2. Allow the THA to reach the temperature setting.
3. Maintain the stable temperature for a period of 24 hours.
4. At the end of the 24 hour period, allow the unit in test to again return to ambient room temperature.
5. Record the room ambient temperature - <u>68.0 F</u>
6. Turn the unit in test to the ON condition, and run the test software as identified in the Software Used In Test. If there are any problems detected, stop the test and go to the FINAL section of this script. Otherwise, turn the system in test to the OFF condition and continue to the next phase.

FINAL
1. If any problems were noted in the previous phases, complete a Trouble Report (Form TR22) and return the unit in test to Engineering with a copy of the Trouble Report.
2. File a copy of the Trouble Report in the unit test report file.
3. If no problems were encountered, place a copy of this test results in the unit test report file.
4. Remove all equipment from the THA chamber.

Appendix E – Sample Market Requirements Document

Radio Frequency Identification Device
Market Requirements

Introduction

In the toll road industry there is a need for identification devices that will allow users of the toll road to bypass toll payment stations by maintaining sufficient funds in a registered account with the toll authority. Such patrons must have a method of being positively identified during the use of the toll facilities. This is the fundamental requirement for such device(s), using the principle of radio frequency identification (RFID).

The U. S. Transportation Administration forecasts the expansion of state sponsored toll roads at the rate of 2,000 miles per year for the next 25 years, with most expansion being found in the metropolitan areas of the East coast and West coast where the greatest road usage is found. The number of daily users can easily exceed 10 million in that time frame, with casual users adding up to 1 million users per day. The anticipated sales for all vendors are estimated at 1.7 million units per year for the mobile device, and 1000 reader devices.

Product Forecast

The product forecast is given in three scenarios, Low, Medium, and High, where the sales forecast depends heavily on product schedule to ship, market penetration for the new product, current participants in the market, customer usability, and product cost. Each of the dependencies are described as follows:

- Schedule – Product must be in inventory, with all Product testing, Manufacturing testing, and Quality acceptance completed prior to Announce and Ship. All of the required testing, tooling, documentation, and compliance testing must be completed within 12 months.

- Market Penetration – The new product Medium forecast is anticipated to capture 7% of the annual market the first year, growing at a 2% annual growth rate for a 5 year period, yielding a 15% market share at the end of the 5th year. For the Low forecast, this will use 5% the first year and 1% per year growth for a total market penetration of 10%, and a High forecast of 9% and 3% per growth for a total market penetration of 21%.
- Competition (Market Share) – AutoID (55%), AutoTag (30%), TollTag (12%), others (3%).
- Customer Usability – Mobile devices must require no customer efforts other than mounting the device as required by the Toll Authority, using double-stick tape, Velcro, or other prescribed method (no wires, screws, bolts, etc.). Readers must have replacement parts easily replaced with no special tool requirements, test equipment, or other special devices. Readers must be installed by a trained technician without extensive support.
- Product Cost – For the Low forecast, the mobile device cost is greater than $5.00 and the reader cost greater than $1200. For the Medium forecast, the mobile device cost is $3.50 to $4.99 and the reader between $1000 and $1199. For the High forecast, the mobile device cost is less than $3.50 and the reader less than $1000.

Revenue Forecast

The revenue forecast is based on the predicted sales forecasts and cost requirements. For the five year period this should yield the annual revenue illustrated in Table 1.

Forecast	Unit	Year 1	Year 2	Year 3	Year 4	Year 5
Low		5%	6%	7%	8%	9%
	Tags @$5.00	85,000	102,000	119,000	136,000	153,000
		$425,000	$510,000	$595,000	$680,000	$765,000
	Readers @ $1200	50	60	70	80	90
		$60,000	$72,000	$84,000	$96,000	$108,000
Medium		7%	9%	11%	13%	15%
	Tags @ $4.00	119,000	153,000	187,000	221,000	255,000
		$476,000	$612,000	$748,000	$884,000	$1,020,000
	Readers @ $1100	70	90	110	130	150
		$77,000	$99,000	$121,000	$143,000	$165,000
High		9%	12%	15%	18%	21%
	Tags @ $3.00	153,000	204,000	255,000	306,000	357,000
		$459,000	$612,000	$765,000	$918,000	$1,071,000
	Readers @ $900	90	120	150	180	210
		$81,000	$108,000	$135,000	$162,000	$189,000

Table 1 – Forecast revenue for 5 year period

The revenue summary is given in Table 2 for the data from Table 1.

Forecast	Tag Totals	Reader Totals	Revenue Total
Low	595,000	350	$3,395,000
	$2,975,000	$420,000	
Medium	935,000	550	$4,345,000
	$3,740,000	$605,000	
High	1,275,000	750	$4,500,000
	$3,825,000	$675,000	

Table 2 – Forecast Total Revenue for 5 year period

User Community

Besides the toll user community, the technology will also find applications such as community parking lots, university parking lots, airport parking lots, airport access control, weigh station bypass, toll tunnels, transportation gate control, and similar applications. The additional opportunities could more than double the revenue given in Table 2.

Device Features

Tag –
- Approximate size, 3x4x1 inch (must not interfere with driver's view)
- Must transmit to distances of 100 feet minimum
- Operating frequency from 900MHz to 5.3GHz
- Operating speeds to 100 mph
- No shadow for vehicles separated by at least 10 feet
- If battery operated, battery must have 3 year life considering 4 reads per day
- If battery operated, battery replaceable by user (data retention required during replacement process)
- No wires required for power
- Installable by neophyte user
- ID must be a 48 bit unique identifier
- Operating temperature from -40F to +120F
- Water tight container
- Read/Write capability for user account summary and/or time mark

Reader –
- Approximate size, 18x18x6 inches
- Must have multiple mount methods (pole, frame, etc.)
- Operated from commercial power, 50/60Hz, 120/240V
- Must be able to detect tags to distances of 100 feet
- Must be able to correspond with multiple tags to speeds of 100 mph
- Must provide tag read/write communications
- Operating frequency between 900MHz and 5.3GHz
- Water tight container
- Operating temperature from -40F to +120F
- Failing units must be field repairable (replacement FRU technology)

- No special mounting, installation, or repair tools
- No special test equipment for field technicians

Reliability

Tag –
- Mean Time Between Failure – 5 years expected, 3 years required
- Mean Time To Repair – 5 minutes for battery replacement, 2 minutes for tag replacement

Reader –
- Mean Time Between Failure – 10 years expected, 5 years required
- Mean Time To Repair – 15 minutes expected, 30 minutes required

Language Support
All documentation will be available in English, French, German, Spanish, Chinese, and Japanese. Any other language requirements will be handled through the Request for Price Quote (RPQ) process.

Compliance
Both tags and readers will comply with the following regulatory agency requirements:
Underwriter Labs (UL)
Canadian Standards Agency (CSA)
Compliance Europe (CE)
European Union (EU)
International Standards Organization (ISO)
American National Standards Institute (ANSI)
Federal Communications Commission (FCC)
and others as may be identified by specific country and/or user requirements.

Appendix F – Sample Engineering Specification

Product X Specification

Revision: NR
Date: XX/XX/XXXX

Signature Page

Reviewed by: _____   _____
             Name, Title, email   Date

Reviewed by: _____   _____
             Name, Title, email   Date

Reviewed by: _____   _____
             Name, Title, email   Date

Reviewed by: _____   _____
             Name, Title, email   Date

Table of Content

A complete Table of Content would be inserted into the document here.

1.0 SCOPE

This section provides a verbal description of what the product is and its intended use.

1.1 General

This specification establishes the design, construction, performance, and test requirements for the Product X System, (herein referred to as the TollWay (acronym· or shortened name).

Additional descriptive paragraphs can be added if needed for special classification, designation of alternate versions or other material part of a top-level description.

2.0 APPLICABLE DOCUMENTS

This section is a list of documents that are a critical part of understanding the item or requirements imposed on the item. Every document listed must have a text reference in the body of the specification further describing and limiting how it is to be applied. Conversely, no document is to be referenced in the specification unless it is listed here.

2.1 Government Documents.

This is where to put MIL-specs, MIL-STDs, NASA, EU specifications and so forth. Be sure to include the revision level and date.

2.2 Industry Documents.

This is where to put ANSI, ASTM, ASME, IEEE, ISO, UL/CSA, API, Company specifications and so forth. Both this section and government documents can be divided up into logical subcategories, i.e. classical testing requirements, safety requirements, shipping requirements, environmental requirements, and so forth.

3.0 REQUIREMENTS

This is the major section of the document. It is requirements and not methods. The definition here must be able to be substantiated via testing and/or inspection.

3.1 Item definition

A more detailed description than provided in SCOPE. The inclusion of an illustration, block diagram, or other illustrative material is appropriate. A reference to the intended use and user should also be included.

3.1.1 Illustrations or Functional Block Diagram

Helps define input and output requirements covered in Section 3.1.1 diagram.

3.1.2 Physical Characteristics

Mountings, size, materials, and so forth should be described here.

3.1.3 Electrical

Includes voltage, frequency, loading, and isolation requirements, including ranges permitted (and under what conditions, if any).

3.2 Characteristics

This is the focal point of the REQUIREMENTS section. The outline may be expanded as needed to provide the necessary depth of explanation. State requirements in the imperative "shall".

3.2.1 Performance Characteristics

A quantitative statement of how the item does what it does. For a power supply it would be current, voltage, and efficiency. Times like rise times, fall times, and transients are defined here. Leakage (fluid or current) is usually defined here. It is a good idea to start with a previous specification for a similar item to get ideas for all that may need to be in this section. Curves, truth tables, and functions may be better than words for these requirements.

3.2.2 Physical characteristics

This is the place for the envelope drawing that shows size and general configuration. Sensitive areas, keep-out zones, and dynamic envelopes should be defined here. The mass, mass moment of inertia, center of mass, and natural frequency requirements can be defined here. Any unusual orientation requirements (e.g. "this side up") can be defined here. Location requirements for electrical connectors or tube- fitting interfaces should be defined. Visual indicators or inspection zones or tool access zones should be identified. Requirements for service and maintenance access, and any special needs for operator controls and access should also be included here.

3.2.3 Environments

This section is for all external entities the item must withstand. Customers may impose these with an "Environmental Requirements Document". Margins should be added beyond hard environmental limits that would damage the item. Generally, environmental requirements will be written at the system level and apply to all sub- systems.

3.2.4 Natural Environments

Anything that is relevant to the product that may occur in the natural world, either prior to use or during use. Words like "The item shall meet the requirements of this specification during and after exposure to any combination of any of the following natural environments. The item may be packaged to preclude exposure to any environments that would affect the design.".

Typical environments include (but are not limited to):
- External Pressure, remember barometric and transportation in unpressurized aircraft. Also rate of pressure change.
- Temperature including both operating and non-operating. Some special temperatures may include freezing points of consumables like fuels.
- Humidity
- Salt spray or other corrosives
- Lightning
- Magnetic fields

3.2.5 Induced Environments

Anything that is relevant to the product caused by human-made objects, either prior to use or during use. Some words like "The item shall meet the requirements of this specification during and after exposure to any logical combination of the following natural environments.".

Typical environments include (but not limited to):

- Mechanical shock, including transportation and use. Amplitude and number of shocks can be defined in either the time domain or frequency domain.
- Vibration, including transportation and use. Amplitude as a function of frequency is the usual format. Duration is a key part of this requirement.
- Acoustic input and output
- Load factors and acceleration
- External Pressure, remember barometric and transportation in unpressurized aircraft. Also rate of pressure change.
- Temperature during operation. Also thermal cycling and thermal/vacuum.

3.2.6 Electromagnetic interference (EMI)

The product shall met the EMI requirements for class *xxx* equipment as specified in MIL-STD-461 (or other standards listed in the REFERENCE section), except for *yyy* limits shall be modified as shown in Figure *zzz*.

Emissions refer to EMI that originates in the unit that can negatively affect other things. Susceptibility refers to unexpected negative effects on the unit that are caused by emissions from some other source. Self- susceptibility is a special case when electrical noise created by the unit triggers an unexpected effect within the unit. EMI can be "conducted" along power or signal wires or "radiated".

Magnetic fields are another category controlled by the MIL-STD. Testing methods are usually defined by an associated methods documents. Other parts or sub- paragraphs in this section deal with electrical bonding (specified minimum resistance) between different subassemblies, EMI gasket and screen materials, grounding, lightning transients, and shielding.

3.3 Quality conformance methods

The supplier shall verify all requirements of Section 3 by inspections, demonstrations, tests, or analyses as follows:

- Inspection. Inspection is a method of verification consisting of investigation, without the use of special laboratory appliances or procedures, to determine compliance with requirements. Inspection is generally nondestructive and includes (but is not limited to) visual examination, manipulation, gauging, and measurement.

- Demonstration. Demonstration is a method of verification that is limited to readily observable functional operation to determine compliance with requirements. This method shall not require the use of special equipment or sophisticated instrumentation.

- Analysis. Analysis is a method of verification, taking the form of the processing of accumulated results and conclusions, intended to provide proof that verification of a requirement has been accomplished. The analytical results may be based on engineering study, compilation or interpretation of existing information, similarity to previously verified requirements, or derived from lower level examinations, tests, demonstrations, or analyses.

- Test. Test is a method of verification that employs technical means, including (but not limited to) the evaluation of functional characteristics by use of special equipment or instrumentation, simulation techniques, and the application of established principles and procedures to determine compliance with requirements. In later stages functional operation under varied conditions may be appropriate, and be defined in a separate test plan.

Index

H

Health and Safety Engineering 57
Human Factors 7, 10, 43, 44, 45
Human Resources 48

I

IEEE 50, 64, 74, 97
imagination 90, 91, 92
industrial engineer 15
Information Systems 61, 77
Information Technology 55, 77
innovation 92
installation 43, 45
Intellectual Property 83
invention 93
ISO 35, 39, 57, 74

L

Lab Testing 27
Lao Tzu 7
Legal 94
LSR 30

M

maintainability 28, 31
maintenance 43, 45
maintenance personnel 45
manager 1, 2, 3, 47
manufacturability 28, 31, 34
Manufacturing 22, 74, 78, 94
Manufacturing Engineering 15, 51, 55, 56, 58
manufacturing variability 27
Marketing 19, 23, 69, 73, 74, 79, 94
market requirement 19, 20, 36, 41
Mask Works 84
material specification 60, 62, 63, 64, 75, 77
Mechanical Engineering 14
mentor 49, 97, 99, 100, 101
morals 97, 98
MTBF 21
MTTR 21

N

NASA 11
NSPE 97

O

OBTW 94
operating environment 31
operating instructions 42
operation 43
operator 45, 54, 57
Other Protections 88

P

paper 47, 70
paradigm 4, 5, 7, 91
part variability 41
patent 84, 85, 87, 88, 89
petroleum engineer 15
petroleum industry 14
PLD 30
PLT 30
power engineer 13
power industry 15
presentation 51, 68, 69
procedure 11, 25, 39, 47, 53, 54, 56, 57, 58, 79
process 56, 65, 94
product champion 78
product engineer 27, 78, 79
product manager 78
Product Planner 51
product specification 19, 22, 36
Product Test 11, 13, 17, 20, 21, 22, 25, 27, 30, 31, 32, 35, 41, 55
programming 10, 11, 14, 27, 43, 71, 77, 85, 88
proof of performance 30
provisional patent 86
Purchasing 94

Q

Quality 21, 22, 39, 40, 41, 42, 55, 57, 60, 73, 74
Quality Assurance 20, 39

R

RAS 33
regression test 27, 28
reliability 28, 31, 33
remote collaboration 73
reports 47, 50, 52
requirement 22, 23, 25, 26, 28, 31, 35,
    41, 42, 45, 60, 74, 75
RFI 30
RFID 37
robot 10, 90, 93, 94

S

Safety 73
Sales Engineer 51
sensitivity 1, 2
serviceability 23, 33
service mark 84, 87
SME 97
software testing 31
solution 90, 99, 100
specification 25, 26, 28, 31, 41, 42, 45,
    52, 60, 61, 62, 63, 74, 78, 79
standard 22, 36, 57, 58, 59, 64, 74, 75
survivability 27
SWOT 21
system 10, 11, 31
system test 32

T

TAC 12, 48
TAC/ABET 12, 48
technical specification 22, 35
technical writing 11, 49
technicians 43
Test Engineering 16, 17, 51
testing 10, 26, 41
test plan 19, 27, 31, 35
test script 27, 29, 30, 31
THA 30, 35
trademark 84, 86, 87
Trade Secrets 84, 88
training 44, 54, 55, 56
truth-in-advertising 32

U

UL 74
UL/CSA 22
usability 8, 27, 28, 31, 32
user 20, 21, 22, 23, 26, 27, 28, 31, 32,
    34, 41, 42, 43, 45, 51, 61
USPTO 84, 85, 87

V

vendor 40, 41, 42, 60, 66, 73, 77, 79,
    94

W

web based 61
writer 43, 52